BILLION DOLLAR DIMEBAG

BILLION DOLLAR DIMEBAG

AN INSIDER'S ACCOUNT OF AMERICA'S LEGALISH CANNABIS INDUSTRY

JACKSON D. TILLEY

Post Hill
PRESS

A POST HILL PRESS BOOK

Billion Dollar Dimebag:
An Insider's Account of America's Legalish Cannabis Industry
© 2019 by Jackson D. Tilley
All Rights Reserved

ISBN: 978-1-64293-269-0
ISBN (eBook): 978-1-64293-270-6

Cover art by Ellen Bruss Design
Interior design and composition by Greg Johnson, Textbook Perfect

Post Hill Press
New York • Nashville
posthillpress.com
Published in the United States of America

For Michael,
who not only accepts my neuroses,
but loves me because of them.

And to Mom, Dad, and Meme,
for giving them to me in the first place.

"Smoking even one marijuana cigarette is equal in brain damage to being on Bikini Island during an H-bomb blast."

—RONALD REAGAN

"I experimented with marijuana a time or two, and I didn't like it, and I didn't inhale, and I never tried again."

—BILL CLINTON

"When I was a kid I inhaled frequently. That was the point."

—BARACK OBAMA

Table of Contents

Preface

All kids snoop. It occurs to me that rummaging through a sibling's belongings is just something children of a certain age do. I'm not sure if it's the result of simple curiosity or something more complex—a deep-rooted desire to better understand the private lives of those close to us. Whatever the reason, I'm nosy. I always have been and likely always will be. If you were to take a sample of my DNA, blow it up 100 times its normal size, and project it onto a screen, you would undoubtedly see that each step on my genetic ladder is earmarked with a proclivity for meddling.

If memory serves, the year was 2004 and my family had just moved into a new house. It was on the opposite side of town—the ritzy side where golf courses and private schools were on every corner rather than the grilled corn carts that had adorned our prior neighborhood. My older brother had taken over the unfinished basement, a sort of pubescent man-cave, if you will. The walls were covered with Bob Marley posters and the floors with used Kleenex— the trappings of a room any sixteen-year-old could call home.

One day, congenital yenta that I am, I made my way to the basement to have a quick look around. My brother was out, but that didn't keep me from tiptoeing down each step, one by one. My father had built my brother's bed for him when he was a young child, and beneath the frame were two drawers. I suppose instinct grabbed hold of me and I pulled them open. The drawers were filled with everything you'd expect a sixteen-year-old boy to possess—old *Playboy* magazines (gross), football gear (boring), and something wrapped up in an old T-shirt (intriguing). I couldn't place what exactly it was. At a sensory level, I certainly recognized the stale smoke smell. But there was another scent that reminded me of my uncle's office (an odor I now know as ditch weed). I felt around a bit more until the foreign object finally emerged. It was a bright blue bong. I'm not quite sure I even knew what it was for, but I certainly recognized it as evil.

I grabbed it and sprinted up the stairs like an Olympian, my eyes welling with tears as I thought about how I was going to break the news to my unsuspecting mother. "Cole is doing something awful!" I screamed. I held the bong up in the air as if it were Simba and I was starring in *The Lion King* ("*Nants ingonyama bagithi baba*"). I don't think she had any idea how to react. She was probably as stunned as I was, though her shock came more from my reaction than the actual contraband I was holding. She was, after all, a child of the '60s, and I now know that she was no stranger to cannabis and its attendant paraphernalia. She put the bong in a cabinet and told me she'd speak with my brother, and I walked away feeling some satisfaction in knowing I was protecting my older brother from the perils of pot.

Looking back on it, I don't think I had any real concept of what it meant to smoke marijuana, aside from what I had learned in D.A.R.E. (Drug Abuse Resistance Education) during middle school health class. For me, it boiled down to a pretty simple concept—drugs are evil and, by extension, so too are the people who use them. I cried to my mom for hours after I found these instruments of personal destruction hidden in the bowels of our home like fire and brimstone of the very depths of hell.

I knew from that moment that I would *never* use cannabis or support anyone who did. Maybe I didn't know it was called cannabis at the time, but I surely wasn't going to propagate the notion that "doing pot" was harmless. It was clear to me that weed and the people who used it would eventually end up in jail, or worse, the principal's office. That wasn't the life for me. No. I was a straight-A student and had earned the trust of my parents and peers through years of determination and hard work. Smoking marijuana and being successful were mutually exclusive. You simply could not have one with the other.

Then came college.

I quickly realized that recreational drugs were widely used in every social circle imaginable—marijuana even more so. I was jolted into a world where people could casually smoke weed while still holding down a job, going to the gym, or getting straight As in school. My view on what it meant to be a so-called drug user had been flipped upside down. I suppose that's why they call it an education. What also became apparent was that I simply couldn't drink or do drugs like other people. For me, one was too many and a hundred was never enough. Of course, this didn't become apparent until much later in my life, and not before a rehab stint in Malibu and eight years of therapy. But, hey, at least I got a few great years out of it.

I didn't graduate from college with the intention of joining a cannabis company. It sort of just…happened. Like many young people, diploma in hand, I emerged into the job market without a clue of what I wanted to do for a living. I'd taken interviews at advertising agencies and marketing firms, both types of businesses that would gladly accept a communications degree as the price of entry. None were a good fit. I'd heard about a company called O.penVAPE and went in for an interview. They hired me as an intern, and the rest, as they say, is history.

Fast-forward five years and cannabis and its various derivatives are legal in some form in thirty-three states, and 62 percent of Americans support federal legalization. All of this, and yet drug-addicted children aren't raining down from the sky. Our worst fears have not been realized. In fact, the great social experiment—legalizing marijuana—has proven to be one of the biggest tax generators in modern history. Petty crime rates have declined, teen use has dropped significantly (according to a study by the National Institute on Drug Abuse which found that after legalization efforts began in 2012, teen use dropped off and has stayed at the same level since), and most of all, people seem happy. The current American political climate is—pardon my language—monumentally fucked. Cannabis could very well prove to be the white knight that saves us from ourselves. After all, wouldn't almost anyone be just a bit happier if they were a little stoned?

Whether you consume cannabis or not (and I don't, but more on that later), the last ten years have shown that it's not going to disappear. Cannabis is on the verge of blossoming into a $150 billion industry over the next five years, and I suspect it will surpass alcohol sales shortly after that. Once we get past our hang-ups about what it means to be a cannabis consumer, it becomes clear that it really can be an industry just like any other. It took me the better part of a decade to overcome my own prejudices and embrace what cannabis use can look like in the twenty-first century.

My story is not unique. My goal is not insurrection. I simply want to change the hearts and minds of those who question personal freedom when it comes to the use of cannabis. I look forward to the day when I don't have to argue with strangers about the glory of a regulated cannabis market. Until then, consider this book my ultimate tool in the battle for mass persuasion, offering an education on a massive, mysterious new market. It's an inside look at the characters, history, and science behind the next great American industry, one that has long lived in the shadows. It's time to shine a light and open a dialogue that will bring cannabis further into the mainstream at last.

CHAPTER 1

Colorado Gold

"Marijuana is legal in Colorado. Let's play 'Hardball.'" Chris Matthews knows how to sell an intro. When I think about election night 2012, I can still hear his voice as he panned from a results cutaway to his own talking head. I took a celebratory bong hit and sunk a little bit deeper into our tan, microsuede couch that had been lovingly broken in over the prior two years. Not only had Barack Obama won a second term, but Colorado had approved Amendment 64, which meant that our state would be the guinea pig for "adult-use cannabis." (That's the phrase most frequently used in 2018, as "recreational marijuana" carries with it some unfortunate connotations.)

At the time, it didn't seem like a big deal that marijuana had become legal for adult-use in Colorado. I had been smoking weed since my freshman year of college, and the only thing easier than buying marijuana was the trip to the doctor to obtain the medical card allowing me to do so. Prior to 2012, many Coloradans could stumble into a clinic, check a box on a form describing their self-diagnosed ailment, and walk out with a prescription for cannabis. This concept was not novel. Indeed, California had been the real pioneer in medical marijuana, offering those same benefits some twenty years prior. But I digress. To us, a group of bright-eyed college students earning our degrees at the University of Cannabis, er, Colorado, in Boulder, it felt like we had struck gold.

The measure passed with almost 54.8 percent of Coloradans voting in favor of it, most of whom I doubt had any concept of what it would mean not just for the state, but for the nation as a whole. It was the first domino in a long line that would eventually fall and prove that Colorado's "great experiment" was not just some harebrained idea conjured up while passing a joint, but an immense step forward in the battle for personal freedom across the country. It was a fight for more than just marijuana; it was a leap forward in creating what history will prove as one of the greatest American industries. Amendment 64 had found its way onto the ballot in much the same way as any other initiative: a group of dedicated individuals joined forces to convince voters that legalized marijuana would benefit the masses, not just the stoner archetype that had been drilled into our psyches for decades. At its core, the amendment was about revitalizing Colorado's economy and providing much needed tax revenue for a state that had struggled to be known for anything beyond skiing and Coors Light, a beer that tastes like someone else may have drunk it before it was canned.

While there were certainly large numbers of cannabis consumers already living in Colorado, one of the most appealing aspects of the bill was that $40 million of any tax revenue generated by cannabis sales would be earmarked for public schools. Let people get high in the privacy of their own homes, help erode the black market, and generate taxes for the state that will be used, in some instances, to benefit education. These taxes are not placed directly into schools' operating budgets, but broken up into several verticals and spread out across the state. For the 2017–18 school year, the funds went to things like substance-abuse programs, grants for early literacy programs, and new construction for school building projects. Who could argue with that? Well, lots of people apparently. Around 2011, a special interest group opposed to the proposed legalization of cannabis popped up in Colorado that strategically placed ads with a clear message: smoking weed is bad for our kids, it's bad for our community, and it offers no benefits whatsoever. What a bunch of squares.

A "No On 64" flyer was circulated throughout Colorado that made the viewpoint of anti-cannabis groups abundantly clear. It posed a question no one had bothered to ask: Why vote no on Amendment 64? It conflicts with federal law and, according to their anecdotal research, promotes increased use among teens. My apologies in advance if I insult MAEC, or "Mothers Against Eating Cheetos" (a special interest group nickname that I've just made up), but legalized cannabis would not harm children and would instead support them through tax revenue for their schools. History would eventually show that legalized marijuana decreased the instances in which teens smoked weed, because a regulated infrastructure was created to prevent such underage use. Hindsight is always 20/20 of course, so it's easy to poke holes in the arguments of years past. That's not to say that legalized marijuana doesn't still have plenty of naysayers in Colorado, but they have mostly been silenced by the reality of what the regulated cannabis market has produced for communities.

So, after a great deal of fanfare and fearmongering, cannabis became legal in Colorado for those twenty-one and older. Thus began the next chapter in the state's history, one marked not by toddlers asking for bongs instead of Cabbage Patch Kids, but a new era of commerce, innovation, tax revenue, and, of course, more weed and dispensaries than we knew what to do with.

I continued to frequent the dispensary throughout college, and in hindsight, I think I often took for granted what a unique moment in history it was. For the first time, young people in America had the choice between two legal intoxicants: Do I want to visit the liquor store for some cheap vodka and Coors Light, or should I head to the dispensary next door for some OG Kush and an edible? The answer for me was both. As a twenty-seven-year-old Colorado native, I have been able to just go and get weed whenever I wanted it for my entire adult life. Sure, this may have been the case for others in places without a regulated market too, but the difference is that I faced no legal ramifications for getting high at my leisure. Colorado is a veritable cornucopia of cannabis, and whatever your particular inclination, a solution exists. Craving infused beef jerky? We have that. Got a hankering for white chocolate filled with pop rocks? Head over to The Farm and pick up a few. Boulder is filled with dispensaries with names more akin to farm-to-table restaurants than weed shops, and boy, for someone who charged their entire existence to their parents' credit cards throughout college, that was a blessing sent from above. "No, Mom, The Clinic is where I went to get my TB shot!"

A group of us from work were recently in Australia with the owners of a hemp beverage company called Chill, It's Legal. As we sat around a tapas restaurant on Sydney Harbour discussing the differences between our two markets, they shared with us the tagline for one of their products: "When's the last time you had a first time?" The table burst into laughter, as it was such a poignant commentary on what it means for so many consumers to try cannabis. I was reminded of my first time (and no, not the one at age sixteen when I tried to convince myself that having a girlfriend was a good idea during a particularly awkward game of seven minutes in heaven). Rather, I was taken back to my first day in college.

Boulder, Colorado—twenty-five square miles surrounded by reality, as it's lovingly referred to—is a solid contender for the closest thing on Earth to utopia (so long as you're a well-off Democrat). I walked onto campus in the fall of 2010 having never had a sip of alcohol, let alone anything else. I'd held true to my puritanical values that had been seemingly instilled in me out of thin air. I found some friends and decided I'd get the full college experience by going to a "cool" party. "I'm cool! I'm cool!" I whispered to myself in the mirror, acting as my very own hype-man, sweat dripping from my palms and soaking through a teal Hollister shirt. (2010 was a rough year for my personal fashion sense). A group of us trekked to The Hill, the area where many students live during their four (or five, or six, or seven) years as an undergraduate.

The party was being hosted by a friend of a friend with a nickname too absurd to repeat. Within ten minutes, I had a beer in my hand, and I have to tell you, I hated it. My drink of choice would later become a vodka soda with a splash of cran, like any respectable gay man, but back then I made do with beer. An hour passed and I found myself railing a line of coke off a mirror, imagining I was a 1980s power-banker who needed a little pick-me-up before a board meeting. (*American Psycho* is a favorite film, if that wasn't already obvious). Fast-forward another hour, and there I was face-to-face with my old foe, the dingy glass object last spotted in my brother's bedroom drawer some ten years earlier. This bong was a bit different though. It was four feet tall, and I had to stand on an ottoman to properly position myself above it. My new friend lit the bowl for me, and I inhaled as if I was sucking the wind out of a tornado. I cleared the bong, the room cheered, and someone gave me their hat as a prize. I still have it. Doing drugs makes you cool—that was my first lesson in college, before classes had even begun.

You might be thinking that my experience sounds an awful lot like what the opponents of Amendment 64 were so concerned about, that in using cannabis, people open themselves up to the seedy underbelly of drug use. The truth is, that was just the first red flag in a long personal history of addiction, a disease that neither I nor the professionals who have treated me blame on cannabis use, but more on all of that later.

Like my own experience with drugs, regulated cannabis use is awash with contradictions. When marijuana is legal, kids have a harder time gaining access to it. Cannabis use becomes normalized, and our cities get healthier. When weed is sold legally on every corner, somehow crime and intoxicated driving rates often go down. If we really are to push ourselves into the next societal dimension, we have to cast aside our prior notions about what it means to be a cannabis consumer in the twenty-first century. There is no better example than Colorado when it comes to the merits of a market in which cannabis is legal. It all boils down to five basic changes that happen when communities rally to support ending the war on cannabis and providing safe and reliable access to it: tax revenue, increased job opportunities, decreased crime rates, keeping drugs away from our kids, and allowing our police force to focus on crimes more important than cannabis possession. That's it. I can't think of another issue that resonates more with people, and for good reason. Who doesn't wish for safer neighborhoods for our children, who can excel without worrying their parents the moment they leave their line of sight. Oh yeah, and buckets of money too.

I'm back living in Colorado some six years after marijuana became legal, and all I can see are streets paved with green. The state is raking in tax dollars, cities are seeing long-vacant real estate snatched up at higher premiums than ever, highways are being expanded, and condos are popping up faster than developers can slap trendy names on them. Since 2014, Denver has had more active cranes than almost any other city in America. What does that tell you about the benefits of cannabis on a community? Cannabis is a sin, some will tell you, so why not tack on a sin surcharge and let the citizens cash the check?

Let's start at the highest level and work our way down: tax revenue. In 2017, Colorado surpassed half a billion dollars in taxes generated by cannabis. Let that number soak in for a moment. More than half a *billion* dollars in taxes, simply by allowing adults to purchase something they'd been buying tax-free for the better part of a century. It's important to note that though that number is impressive, it accounts for just over 1 percent of the state's annual budget. I say this not to minimize the effects of legalization, but to point out that the economic improvements don't simply come from state and local taxes. By legalizing marijuana, Colorado didn't just slap a tax on a consumer good, but rather created an entirely new industry. It's one that increases tourism and motivates transplants to call Colorado home.

Colorado has sold roughly $4 billion in cannabis since 2014, according to data collected by BDS Analytics, but that is just the tip of the green iceberg. In 2017 alone, 70,000 people moved to Colorado, the bulk of them choosing to call Denver home, much to the chagrin of locals who loathe seeing California license plates clogging up the freeways. That's just shy of 200 people per day relocating to a state that had largely stagnated in terms of innovative industries, often being overshadowed by places like Silicon Valley, Los Angeles, and New York. Even I contributed to that influx, leaving the state in 2014 only to return in 2018. Property values have largely increased as well, creating a secondary revenue stream for the state and its residents. Real estate prices have hit an all-time high, thanks in large part to a boom in those chasing the so-called green rush. Housing prices are up 6 percent in the last year, according to a study by Walter Mayer, Yanling Mayer, and Cheng Cheng in the journal *Economic Inquiry.*

When discussing teen drug use in Colorado, I'm often reminded of Helen Lovejoy, the wife of Reverend Lovejoy on *The Simpsons*, whose constant refrain of "won't somebody *please* think of the children?" seemingly echoes in the minds of concerned Colorado parents. The worst fears of what would become of Colorado's kids have proven to be unfounded. In the post-legalization era, teen use of marijuana has fallen to its lowest rates in history, according to a 2017 federal study. Just 9 percent of Colorado teens aged 12–17 report using cannabis, down from 12 percent in 2013. This decline took place in an environment where a well-regulated industry enforced harsh penalties on dispensaries found selling to minors.

And what about crime rates? For Colorado, it's sort of like the candy drawer in my apartment that my friends raid after a particularly long hit off a vape pen—something of a mixed bag. In an interview with the *Colorado Statesman*, Marijuana Industry Group Executive Director Kristi Kelly said, "The Denver, Aurora and Edgewater police departments have not shown any link between violent crime and marijuana. In fact, the statistics trend in the opposite direction." Overall, most studies seem to agree that overall crime rates are down around 6 percent since 2009. It's not clear if there's a link between the decrease in crime and the legalization of cannabis, but if the police force isn't bogged down with writing tickets for petty cannabis possession, they have more time to devote to more consequential crime. In a study published in *Police Quarterly*, researchers found that "models show no negative effects of legalization and, instead, indicate that crime clearance rates for at least some types of crime are increasing faster in states that legalized than in those that did not." I hope we can all agree that focusing on crimes like robbery and driving under the influence should take precedence over busting college kids for smoking weed in their dorm parking lot. (To the University of Colorado campus police: I hope you're reading this.)

In just six years, Colorado established itself as a model for what it means to have a cannabis market with the full support of its regulators. With Colorado adding more than 18,000 new jobs in 2015 alone, it's become increasingly apparent that creating an infrastructure to buy and sell cannabis benefits regular people. I should probably note my own bias, that having been gainfully employed since 2015 by one of the largest cannabis companies in the world, I have a somewhat unique take on the glories of a regulated market.

All of these statistics may paint a glowing picture of the uniformity of minds across Colorado, but that couldn't be further from the truth. Just last year, I was driving down Broadway in Denver, a street that's known as "the green mile" thanks to the disproportionately high rate of dispensaries who call it home, when I saw a billboard. In huge green letters, it asked "Can Pot Kill Me?" and directed onlookers to visit www.CanPotKill.me. The ad was placed by Smart Colorado, a nonprofit formed after the passage of Amendment 64 to "protect the youth" from the many dangers of marijuana. Their website is filled with out-of-context data painting a picture of marijuana use that would seem more fitting in a scene from *Reefer Madness*. One visit showed a landing page with an image of refined cannabis oil and yet another question, "What is dabbing?" They answer their own question (though, frankly, no one asked them to) with something that almost made my Diet Coke spray out my nose. "The crack cocaine of marijuana." I hadn't heard that one before, but I do have to give them points for creativity in the fearmongering department.

Not to be outdone, our company's marketing team promptly purchased the domain www.CanPotKillMe.com, which leads visitors to a landing page embellished with a large "Nope." In a period of American history plagued by misinformation about cannabis use and the problems that stem from it, our greatest asset is reaching out directly to stakeholders and greeting them with concrete evidence, absent the biases that seem so common among those who work tirelessly to undo all the work of longtime activists and a still-novel industry. When one group likens cannabis oil to crack cocaine and another provides data from the National Institutes of Health, you have to ask, who are the real bad guys here? Our job is to present the facts, create a safe and sustainable marketplace, and let the free will of the people make informed decisions about their own minds and bodies.

We've come a long way since that election night in 2012. The microsuede couch has since been tossed into a dumpster after a few too many nights of drunken debauchery, and Colorado has shown it can sell cannabis without the very fiber of our world coming undone. Seven years have passed since voters elected to embark on The Great Experiment (coincidentally, also the nickname for my high school girlfriend) and things seem to be going smoothly. Business is booming, local communities are happy, and condominiums in Denver have trendy names like "Le Cirque" and "The Sugar Cube," names that, by my best guess, could only have been conceived by someone who's high.

CHAPTER 2

The Google of Cannabis

Graduation day. The moment that undergrads all around the country meet with a simultaneous mix of joy and sadness. Joy, of course, that there will never be another test to take, another chemically induced all-nighter to pull, or another carton of menthol cigarettes to smoke during a particularly stressful finals week. (For the record, smoking is a terrible habit and I quit years ago.) And sadness, of course, at coming to terms with the fact that the gravy train has run out of fuel, and soon it will no longer be possible to invoice one's parents for the costs of daily existence. The thought of having to pay for my own drinks or figuring out how to pay rent was almost too much to bear. A shiver runs down my spine to this day, thinking about the rude awakening that came when my parents uttered the most terrifying five-word sentence known to man (second only to "What's this charge at Target?"):

"Time to get a job."

I graduated from college absolutely clueless about how to function in the real world. The human equivalent of a sea cucumber, I was soft, essentially useless, and devoid of any basic understanding of a higher calling. I'd spent the previous four years going to bars five nights a week (Absinthe House for ladies night, The Sink for flip night…) and attending classes five times a month (if I was feeling studious), while wasting a considerable amount of mental effort contemplating how exactly my communications degree would allow me to buy the Bentley I'd had my eyes on. By some miracle, I managed to get good grades, thanks in large part to a resounding moral commitment to working smarter, not harder. They say that there's a key difference between book smarts and street smarts, and I'd always managed to display that very real dichotomy. This is all coming from a man who, until 2015, thought that the proper name for the discount retail chain *Ross,* was *The Ross.* Sheltered doesn't really begin to cover it.

My parents threw a big graduation party for me in my hometown, while a few of my best friends from undergrad set off on a trip to Europe. I wasn't allowed to go, as a result of failing to find some type of postgrad employment. Always the planner, I convinced my parents to let me leave for Europe after the party, so long as I found a job that would be waiting for me upon my return.

I remembered an acquaintance who had left school the year prior was now working for a cannabis startup about an hour away in Denver. I shot him a text explaining my first-world problem: "I can't go on a eurotrip unless I get a job. UGH, life is so unfair!" She hit me back to let me know that her company was looking for interns. "Working for a weed company? I love weed. Sounds perfect." I hopped on Skype, did an informal (read: nepotistic) interview, and a few minutes later emerged from my bedroom, weed smoke billowing from the doorway like a wildfire, with a new title: Marketing Intern.

I spent the following two weeks on the bender to end all benders, hopping from country to country, reminding the United Kingdom—and every other country we visited—why they should count their blessings that Americans formed their own nation. When I returned, I spent a weekend recovering and felt a shock to my system when I realized that I had to go to work on Monday. The new week came and I found myself waking up with a dizzying mix of nervousness and excitement. It was my first real job, and it was working for a marijuana company. I sashayed through the doors of an old brick building in downtown Denver to begin a career in cannabis. Although I didn't know it at the time, my fake-a-job-to-go-to-Europe ploy would soon evolve into a career spent correcting a century's worth of misinformation about cannabis.

My first day at the office was bereft of dignity. Absent any glimmer of real responsibility, I almost quit then and there (and not just because they expected me to *work until the job was done*). Anyone who's had an internship can essentially walk you through the motions of what happens on a typical day: grab coffee, make copies, clean this, organize that, and on and on. My first task was to head to The Container Store to pick up about a dozen plastic bins that would be used to hold empty vaporizer cartridges at the lab. One of the cofounders of the company watched me stumbling through the door, balancing these plastic monstrosities, and promptly offered to help me carry them inside. It was a wildly different experience than any internship I'd ever had before. So foreign a concept, I think I may have actually muttered "Are you sure?" when his hand reached out to assist.

My first week continued on in much the same manner, constantly being reminded that while it looked like a normal corporate office, it was anything but. The Dreamer Room, an area of the office with walls painted so they could be used as whiteboards, was covered with sales figures, ideas for the next great product, and a list of states where the company operated. I stopped in one day after the close of business, and started reading what was in front of me. It looked like a scene from *Good Will Hunting*, every inch of the room had more and more information covering the walls. My eyes were drawn to some sales numbers. I'm certainly no mathematician (I failed algebra twice) but *holy shit, that's a lot of zeros,* I thought.

And just like that, I realized that I'd gotten myself involved in a *real* business. I clearly had my own preconceived notions of what a cannabis business might look like. I thought smoking weed during the day would be allowed, that work ended at 4:20, and that we were all just there to have a good time. How wrong I was. This was a building full of overachievers looking to change the world, to innovate products, and to create sustainable and life-altering success. This wasn't amateur hour. This was O.penVAPE.

Formed in 2012, O.penVAPE was nothing short of revolutionary. The brainchild of several brilliant entrepreneurs, including Jeremy and Amanda Heidl, Chris McElvany, Tim Cullen, and Ralph Morgan, the company's flagship vape pen forever altered the landscape of cannabis consumption. I say brilliant because from a young age, each brought a specific business prowess to what would one day be their ultimate venture. One founder even made his first foray into business from his elementary school lunch line. He'd calculated that by the time each of his classmates had finished buying lunch in the cafeteria, they had a nickel leftover. So he started selling bulk candy for, you guessed it, five cents apiece.

By the time I walked through the doors in 2014, the business had expanded to six states and had already sold its one millionth cartridge; by the end of 2014, they hit two million units. The company followed a tried-and-true model, the Gillette method—making vaporizer batteries cheap and banking on consumers continuing to regularly purchase the cartridges that go along with them. The model seemed to work, and in just two short years, their products were on more than a thousand shelves from Oregon to Maine, and everywhere where cannabis was legal. One thing was clear: people loved to get high, and we were there to make that happen.

The organization ran like a well-oiled machine. CNBC called us "The Google of Cannabis," and as I looked around and saw beer on tap, organic snacks at every turn, and a staple of any culturally significant business—the ping pong table—I couldn't help but agree with them. Teams worked late hours, not because they had to, but because they wanted to. The founders had created something magical, a place where people wanted to work because they could see that what they were doing was changing the world. One of my first weeks at the company was marked by a late-night marathon to finish assembling point-of-sale packaging. The entire office stayed, pizza slices in hand, making pop-up boxes from flattened cardboard cutouts. It's easy to lose sight of the timeline here but only a decade earlier, you'd have been laughed out of the family dining room if you mentioned that your bills were paid by working in cannabis. I'd found my passion by accident, but I guess that's the way it goes for most. I never set out to sell the idea of cannabis to an entire country, but one look around the office and it just made sense.

My first several months were marked by an array of stress, bewilderment, and pure, unadulterated happiness at seeing our collective dream come to life. It may seem peculiar to have drunk the metaphorical Kool-Aid so quickly, but I'd bought what the founders were selling immediately. From day one, I had a deep sense of pride at being a part of an organization whose mission I believed in, and beyond that, it was instantly apparent to me that I'd fallen into an opportunity that only comes once in a lifetime. One particularly hot summer day, I'd foolishly worn a light blue shirt into the office, a faux-pas for anyone who either stressed or produces an abnormal amount of sweat. It just so happens that I fit both those descriptions. I popped into the bathroom and was forced to stuff paper towels into my shirt to sop up the perspiration flooding from under my arms. I emerged feeling only slightly refreshed and quickly forgot about the paper towels wadded into my shirt. Later that day, I dropped off some documents that needed to be signed with one of the executives. When I reached over his desk to hand him a pen, a wad of sweat-soaked paper towel dropped out from my shirt and landed on the carpet with a soft thud. Turning bright red, I tried to think of an excuse for what had just happened. He looked at me and simply said,

"I get it." We were all being put through the wringer. From executive to intern, everyone was there to get things done.

On my first day, I was one of twenty employees working in the office. By the end of that year, we'd nearly doubled in size and office space was at a premium. I posted up at a portable desk in the corner of someone else's office. It was clear that business was booming. In fact, it was growing faster than we could keep up with. The simple truth of my professional upbringing is this: everything I need to know, I learned from the boiler room inside the largest cannabis company in America. The culture was, and continues to be, singular. The bulk of the staff is under the age of thirty, a group of dreamers who aren't used to being told no. And what better fit for this motley crew than a business hellbent on disrupting American industry and creating something entirely new.

At its core, the business functions like any other. We sell consumer goods at fair prices, using time-tested marketing techniques. Colorado was the litmus test to establish whether a family could pay their bills by selling marijuana—legally. I recently rediscovered a company-wide email that marked the start of our monthly "all hands on deck" meetings:

> We all know that nothing comes free in this world. Assuredly, we enter into this union cognizant that a pound of flesh is the price of admission. But unlike my misguided trip to Tijuana during college, the consequences of this venture shall require you to endure neither physical mutilation nor daily infusions of intravenous antibiotics. Instead, the toll we must each pay is to build a successful company in a highly competitive space, with minimal prior precedent, and modest wages. To accomplish this, we must strive to create an enduring culture.

Culture. Since day one, that's been the name of the game. "But what should our culture be?" the email continues, "Hans Magnus Enzensberger analogizes culture to dropping an Alka-Seltzer into a glass—you don't see it, but somehow it does something." The secret sauce of this business isn't limited to innovation, though that, of course, is half the battle. Rather we focus on placing the right people in the right seats and voilà, magic happens. It is a technique that isn't unique to our business or to the cannabis industry as a whole, but it works. That philosophy has remained true to this day, and I can think of no better example than our current leadership team. Four of the highest-ranking members of our company started as interns.

It was now July 2014, and my first two months in the cannabis industry had come and gone. I'd been commuting back and forth from Boulder to Denver each day, greeting my colleagues every morning with an energy and optimism that communicated I was prepared to take over the world. Though I'd really begun to come into my own, I was still very much an intern and hadn't quite grasped the breadth and intensity of what it meant to run a business in a market that's regulated in a manner like no other. My boss had decided to embark on a ritual that all young tech entrepreneurs must undertake—a trip to Burning Man. I'd heard him discussing it in the weeks leading up to it, but didn't think much of it. Some days later, an instant message appeared asking me to come to his office. They needed my cell phone, as the plan was to forward all of his calls to my phone during his absence. Black Rock City, colloquially known as *the playa*, is devoid of cell service and completely cut off from the outside world. He boarded his flight, and within ten minutes my phone began to ring. First, it was every twenty minutes, then every ten, then every minute. I didn't understand what it meant to be busy until that moment. I can still feel the sweat stinging my eyes as a knot formed in my stomach, knowing that with each ring, a punishment was about to be cast upon me like a sadistic Pavlovian experiment.

Ring. "We've got an issue at the lab." *Ring.* "We need more lanyards for the dispensaries." *Ring.* "Your dry cleaning is ready." *Ring.*

"Are you interested in a discounted subscription to HBO? This offer won't last long!" It was the most trying week of my short career. Why on Earth would anyone trust me to handle this level of responsibility?

My boss returned and told me I'd done a great job and they were all very impressed. "Jackson, we'd like to hire you full time." I couldn't believe it. In two months, I'd gone from a low-level intern to an integral part of the team. For the first time in my life, I felt as if I were doing something important, something that would have real impact. *I was involved in something bigger than myself.* I went out that night to celebrate with friends, and I can recall with crystal-clear memory, a resounding sense of accomplishment. Someone had taken a chance on me, and I hadn't let them down. This was what being an adult felt like.

The first month of real work was a blur, a stressful, hazy blur. I'd gotten the day off to go to a private press junket with then-President Obama. After what I'm sure was a lovely speech, I lined up to have a brief meet-and-greet. He shook my hand, offered his thanks for my support, but the only response my brain could muster was "your hands are so soft." He replied with an awkward "Thanks?" and moved on to the next constituent. The days were long, and it was clearly beginning to take its toll. But it was all worth it. The work we were doing was making an impact on the world. We'd recently heard a story of a child with an incurable seizure disorder. Her family was struggling to find a solution and had relocated to Colorado in a last-ditch effort to try cannabis, only to find that CBD products (made from the non-psychoactive part of cannabis) weren't covered by their insurance. They couldn't afford the medication over the long term. Without hesitation, our executive team funded her treatment, and for the first time in her life, she was able to live without frequent grand mal seizures. There's being a business, and then there's being a member of a community; we always opted for the latter. In that short period, we'd already been featured in *Time*, on CNN and MSNBC, and by many other media outlets. I couldn't help but feel that this must've been what it was like during the early days of Facebook.

Things were expanding at a rapid pace. It seemed that each day a new assortment of prospective partners was meeting with us, trying to get a piece of the action. At this point, the company was totally bootstrapped—the owners hadn't taken on a single investor but had instead opted to grow the business organically on their own. I could barely make it through an episode of *Real Housewives* without either nodding off or checking Instagram, so to witness this level of dedication and gumption was awe inspiring. To put it succinctly, my first four months had been nothing short of a religious experience. I'd been given a chance to succeed and to be a part of something bigger, and no matter how tired we all were, we showed up early and stayed late. It started with getting coffee and morphed into greater and greater responsibilities: meetings with ad agencies, securing national press coverage, and generally adopting a "no task too big or too small" policy when it came to the core business. This was the hallmark of a company that was going places.

At this juncture, we had expanded to include operations in Arizona, Maine, Nevada, Massachusetts, and Oregon. The running joke was that we'd sold enough vaporizers that we could get all of America stoned. Recreational marijuana was now legal in Colorado, those over age twenty-one were lining up outside dispensaries to make their first legal purchases, and our products were front and center for the taking. We'd previously merged with another company, Bakked, that focused on cannabis concentrates. Our new mission wasn't just to be a one-stop shop for vaporizers, but to be a house of brands, a first in the cannabis world. With O.penVAPE and Bakked now in the same portfolio, the parent company Organa Brands was formed. Prior to Organa Brands, there had never been an organization in the cannabis world to bring numerous product names under one umbrella for distribution. The company would later be dubbed the P&G of THC thanks to our adoption of this model. This particular business structure has since been repeated by many others in the space, thanks in part to the efficacy of the model in terms of sales and distribution of products. It had long been clear that cannabis wasn't going away, but it wasn't until this point that it became glaringly apparent that our team was on the path to world domination. (In a good way. I swear!)

The lease on my apartment in Boulder was nearing its end, so I began hunting for a new spot to call home a bit closer to the office. One of my bosses had advised me to hold off on signing on a new place but didn't elaborate why. By this point, I'd already been fully indoctrinated, so I heeded his advice without hesitation. Over the next several weeks, there was increased talk of a new market coming online, one in which it was imperative we get a piece. I was sleeping on my best friend's couch, just a block from the office, and going through the motions of corporate life. One particularly groggy morning, I walked into the office and was asked to run out and grab some champagne flutes—a celebration was impending.

I returned to the office with a few cases of brut and several boxes of glassware, when Phantom Planet's "California" started blaring from the office's Sonos system.

As everyone gathered around, the ownership team announced that we'd been awarded a license in what would prove to be our largest market yet. They selected me and three others from the Colorado team to pack up and head west. We were making the great pilgrimage to the promised land, the sun-soaked West Coast, where they were entrusting us to bring Colorado magic to the Golden State. I packed my bags. Sleeping on a couch for the last month suddenly seemed worth it.

California, here we come.

INTERVIEW WITH CHRIS DRIESSEN

Chris Driessen is the Executive Vice President of Sales and Business Development at SLANG Worldwide, the parent company to Organa Brands. The company is publicly traded on the Canadian Securities Exchange, and in addition to being an original partner in Organa Brands, Mr. Driessen sits on the SLANG board of directors. He's responsible for a marked increase in the company's sales, as well as acting as co-lead during the company's merger and subsequent IPO. I wanted to learn a bit more about the early days of the industry, so we sat down to discuss how he got here.

Tell me about your journey. How did you find yourself working in cannabis?

I have always had a passion for cannabis. I reconnected with an old friend, Chris McElvany, who encouraged me to quit my day job selling copy machines and join his new company. After several interviews, the executive committee decided they could not afford me. I promptly wrote back and let the executives know why they couldn't afford "not to hire me." I conducted a final working interview by leading a sales meeting. While conducting the meeting, I noticed that a film crew was there. It turned out to be a news crew capturing footage for their teaser on CNBC. I was wearing a shirt from my old company that was quite recognizable and it was displayed prominently in the clip. My old boss happened to catch the news that night and when I came in the next morning he asked me, "Do you have anything to tell me?" I happily told him I was going to join the cannabis industry. I then immediately contacted the executives to let them know I better be hired! Fortunately, I was hired that week.

Was there ever a moment when you thought, "Fuck, I need to go back to corporate America?"

All the time. Many people think that working in cannabis you are going to work half as hard and make twice as much. While the financial aspect can be rewarding, you can expect to work harder than you ever have before.

One day, a man in a dark suit walked into our reception area, which my office window overlooks. I noticed that our receptionist was getting very uncomfortable with the conversation and walked out to see what was going on. She said that the gentlemen was from the DEA and wanted to have a conversation with whoever was in charge. My heart stopped for at least five seconds. While we strive to follow the letter of the law, it's not often that you engage with federal law enforcement agents. He proceeded to tell me that they were investigating identity theft and fraudulent purchases that had happened on our website. After some digging around he was able to clear the company of being involved and left, never to be heard from again. For a brief few moments, I thought, why the hell did I leave corporate America?

Do you have any doubt that federal legalization is coming?

Nope. The majority of people in the United States think cannabis should be legalized. In fact, the majority of men and women, white, black, and brown, gay and straight, young and old, liberal and conservative, Republicans and Democrats, all support legalizing cannabis. It's rare to see an issue that has this level of broad support from all parts of our country.

What lessons can we learn from Canada?

Canada was smart in that their legalization from a federal level allowed for access to capital from traditional sources like banks, private equity and stock exchanges. Because their government was more progressive on cannabis, they were able to gain a large head start over their American counterparts.

What did your family say when you told them you'd be leaving a corporate job to enter the Wild West that is the regulated cannabis industry?

My parents, who are very progressive, were hesitant at first due to some of my past indiscretions with drugs. They were concerned that it would lead me back to a time in my life when I didn't make the best decisions. In time, they realized this opportunity wasn't a road back to my past, but an opportunity to participate, at a very early stage, in something very special. My in-laws, on the other hand, still would prefer I do something else. They are very conservative and uneasy about the subject. We rarely talk about it.

What's next? What does the future hold for the cannabis space?

The cannabis industry will grow into a mature market once federal legalization happens in the United States. The capital growth potential has become too large, the stakes too high, and the economic and social impact too great to ignore. I think you will see a diversification in all sectors of the industry with the emergence of specialization (think retail, cultivation, manufacturing, CPG, tech, distribution) becoming more and more evolved. I am thankful to be in the manufacturing, distribution and CPG sectors because in the end, brands get the highest multiple in value.

What role do you think you've played in getting the industry to where it is today?

I played a role in how cannabis markets expand, get licensed or acquired and become part of a multistate, now multinational cannabis empire. The systems and processes we put in place to rapidly grow our footprint in a capital-light way, have now become commonplace. It's cool to realize that we were pioneers in how those goals are accomplished.

What's your favorite memory from your time at Organa Brands?

I have had the time of my life, both personally and professionally since joining the cannabis industry and Organa Brands. I wouldn't trade a single day of that journey for the world. Some of my favorite personal memories were on the many trips we've had around the world. Visiting a private island in New Zealand, staying at our friend's home from Green House Seed Company in Ibiza, a crazy weekend in Vegas, and heli-skiing on sales incentive trips are some that come to mind. There are also so many amazing professional memories that I cherish. Some of those include walking through hundreds (if not thousands) of dispensaries, grows, and labs. I have seen cannabis businesses in dozens of countries and always take time to relish in what I get to do for a living. The cannabis industry is filled with dynamic, independent, and first-class people, all united for a cause and a livelihood. It's been very special to have a hand in building that dream for so many people, my company, my family, and myself. Truly, it's been an absolute honor.

CHAPTER 3

This Could Be Heaven
or This Could Be Hell

We packed our bags, loaded them into a truck, and headed straight for California, specifically, Hermosa Beach. I felt as if I'd been catapulted into a live-action version of the Beach Boys discography. I'd asked our graphic designer to photoshop my face onto a promo poster from the *The Hills*. With one tap of a finger, it was live on my Instagram and my new life had been announced to friends and family across the board.

The company leased a house five blocks from the beach. This was to be the new headquarters for our sales and marketing team in the SoCal area. Meanwhile, another team moved to Northern California and found themselves similarly positioned. We wouldn't just be working together, we'd be living together too. In hindsight, we should've pitched it as our very own reality show. What happens when you put four different personalities under the same roof and ask them to expand a business in an area that can only be described as the most fucked up regulatory environment known to man?

Like any great romance, our first few weeks were filled with excitement and promise. One of the company's founders flew out with us to furnish the house, get us settled, and assign us our upcoming tasks. For the most part, we'd be on our own. It helped, of course, that our house was directly across the street from an Albertsons, a dream come true for the burgeoning alcoholic who drooled at the idea of $19.99 Tito's readily accessible at a moment's notice.

For all its struggles with the regulated market, California was the country's first foray into legalized cannabis. A medical-only state at the time I moved there, you needed a prescription in order to obtain cannabis. It felt light-years behind Colorado. The victory for medical marijuana in California had come many years earlier, as Proposition 215, the Compassionate Use Act of 1996. It empowered medical patients to seek cannabis as medicine from registered caregivers, a term coined during the formation of the statute. Proposition 215 was, at its core, about more than just cannabis. It was about love. The story began with Dennis Peron, an activist in San Francisco, who had lost his partner to the HIV/AIDS epidemic that ravaged the nation in the '80s and '90s. (At present, more than thirty-five million have died from HIV/AIDS, making it one of the deadliest outbreaks in history.) The epidemic was first noticed among doctors in San Francisco after seeing an uptick in both Kaposi sarcoma and pneumonia, two telltale signs of the presence of an infection, among young, gay men. Peron had touted the benefits of medical marijuana in treating HIV and AIDS, knowing what many of us now know, that cannabis had long been used in palliative situations, primarily for its pain-relief and antianxiety indications. The Han-era Chinese surgeon Hua Tuo (c. 140–208) is credited as being the first to use cannabis as a pain reliever, mixing it with wine and delivering it to patients prior to surgery. Proponents valued cannabis for its appetite-stimulating abilities, which was invaluable in combating the wasting syndrome many patients experienced in battling HIV/

AIDS. As a result of the loss of his partner, Peron worked to put forth Proposition P, a San Francisco City Ordinance allowing for medical marijuana. It passed with 79 percent of the vote. In doing so, Peron began laying the ground for his future work on Prop 215, the ballot measure that would change the face of California's cannabis laws. In 1996, according to Peron, "the stars aligned for medical marijuana." With a recently elected Democratic president and an increase in pressure on the California assembly, Prop 215, co-written by Peron, passed as a statewide ballot initiative and was signed into law. As a result, medical marijuana became more prevalent across the state.

Coming back to 2014, we encountered two distinct types of cannabis stores in California, those that operated within the letter of the law and those that operated using a much looser interpretation of the state and local statutes. Because of the somewhat lax enforcement in the state, collectives (another term for dispensaries) were largely self-regulated, meaning that the only ones who were fully compliant were those who wanted to be. The collectives followed the laws that best suited them and ignored those that didn't. Take "dab bars," for example. Think of them as an in-store sampling area for consumers. While not officially illegal, many stores didn't allow them because they sensed that they would undoubtedly become illegal (and in 2018, they did). These collectives, so named because patients were required to make a "donation" in order to receive cannabis "free of charge," existed in a legal gray area, where corruption and mismanagement ran rampant. We'd been tasked with getting a handle on the market, and so, with cash in hand, I walked into a doctor's office to obtain the legally required medical card. The paperwork was laughable. Instead of an area to describe the ailment for which I was seeking treatment, I was greeted with a list of boxes to check, any of which would be considered a qualifying illness. Back pain sounded like a good option, so I ticked the box, handed the form over, and spent the next twenty minutes waiting to see a doctor. He emerged from the exam room, and I use that term loosely, and spent the next eight seconds diligently going over my medical history. As it turned out, I did indeed have back pain (he could tell by looking at the way I checked that box), and cannabis was the solution. Medical card in hand, I walked out the front door and into the adjoining collective to buy my first eighth of Cali Kush.

Weeks later, with a list of prospects in hand, our team converged on collectives across the state to take note of what kind of condition the market was in. My new role at the company was acting as a brand ambassador, a position that works to support the sales team without the tedious and exhausting task of using Salesforce, the software equivalent of Ambien. We spent about a week driving up and down the coast, visiting stores that ranged from elaborate to downright horrifying. One thing was for sure, California was no Colorado. There were no tightly regulated storefronts with genteel front desk staff and iPads from which to place orders. California's cannabis infrastructure was, in short, a clusterfuck. In Colorado, we'd grown used to playing by the rules, following the letter of the law, and making sure that we were in compliance with state and local regulations at all times. Because the cannabis market in Colorado was so novel, regulators had taken a heavy-handed approach at enforcement, and as a result, businesses did not dare step out of line for fear of losing their licenses. This was due in large part to the media attention that had been paid to Colorado, as we were acting as something of an experiment for states who may want to follow suit. At that time in California, however, while a few rules existed, very few were followed by many of the operators. Instead, there was a patchwork of city-by-city regulations that would make anyone's stomach turn. (Hey, look at that, another qualifying illness!)

Some weeks later, I found myself outside of a retail store in downtown LA, staring down the barrel of a gun. This collective, a concrete and steel behemoth in the center of the fashion district, was not fucking around. Clearly, something had happened in the history of this particular store to create an environment in which heavy firepower acted as the singular law of the land. The armed guard standing outside the door was at least 250 pounds, all muscle, and six-and-a-half-feet tall. Meekly, I asked, "Can I go inside, please?" He took a look at me and, apparently realizing that a nervous twink from Colorado did not present much of a threat, moved aside. I walked through the front gates and was met with a large, bullet-proof window, similar to what you'd see at a check-cashing counter. They asked to see my ID, then buzzed me through. It was like *Willy Wonka & the Chocolate Factory* if it took place somewhere in the Eastern Bloc: armed guards in every corner, mounds of flower and infused chocolate on display, barred windows covered with black plastic, and a giant table in the middle set up as a dab bar. Dabbing, for those that don't know, involves using a blow torch to heat up a ceramic nail, on which consumers can vaporize a glob of cannabis oil to maximize its effects and uptake time. Smoking weed *inside* a dispensary? This shit would not fly in Colorado. Not only would a store be shut down instantly by the Marijuana Enforcement Division, but their license would be revoked and their products confiscated and destroyed. When people told me California was the Wild West, they weren't joking.

As a team, we were in over our heads. Not because our products weren't superior or because we didn't know what we were doing, but because the regulatory environment was incongruent with the ways in which we were used to operating. Collectives in California had grown accustomed to a certain manner of business, and we just couldn't acclimate. As I'm sure you can imagine, a gay guy in a Brooks Brothers button-down driving a leased BMW full of educational material and promo items was something of an unwelcome sight. We were going to need to change our strategy.

The first two months living in Los Angeles were total hell. Our accounts weren't interested in carrying new products as there were already more than four hundred different brands of vape pens in their ecosystem. Living with colleagues got old quickly. It took the concept of "work never sleeps" and morphed it into the consummate, unavoidable hellscape. Beyond our home life, the professional tasks were tough, and it was our first time being away from the mothership. We weren't on our own in the broadest sense of the term, but we were no longer privy to the morning pep talks from the executive team, which had a more glaring impact than I'd anticipated. I'd never planned on working in sales, but that's what was needed at the time, so I accepted the challenge and faked confidence in the hopes that this alone would carry me across the finish line. It didn't. Things continued to sour in our living situation, and the market was increasingly hostile. I'd recently visited an Orange County collective, only to be literally pushed out the door by a manager who became indignant when I asked if he'd ever consider carrying products that were free of pesticides. I'd set out to change a market and I was failing dramatically.

Chaos was swirling all around me. Not only had I left my happy life in Colorado in search of something more challenging, but I'd quickly devolved from a social drinker and casual drug user into someone from *Intervention*. I worked all day and drank alone all night. It wasn't the stress of work that led me down this path. Rather, the reality was setting in that I'd never given up any of my bad habits from college. I'd found being away from my friends and family incredibly isolating. It was a vicious cycle—I felt alone, so I took a Xanax. I felt sad, so I drank a bottle of wine. I needed energy, so I popped a Ritalin. Then, of course, I felt guilty for all of those actions, and the only reaction was to do more drugs to drown it out. It was clear that this lifestyle wasn't going to be sustainable. But that was a problem for another day. In hindsight, I don't think I truly understood any of my actions, taking drugs to improve my mood, or at least level it out, was just my new normal. It wasn't until I got sober and had a shift in perspective that the cycle became more clear and I was thus able to attempt to break it.

After a particularly long week, I did as many other middle-aged housewife alcoholics (that is, after all, my alter ego) do and checked myself into a spa in Rancho Palos Verdes. I'd decided it wasn't an issue of drug abuse, but simply millennial burnout. What better solution than a gold-leaf body wrap and two days worth of massages? I popped a handful of Xanax, ordered a mimosa, and hunkered down for a few days of pampering. (As an aside, the story that ensues is mostly pieced together from other people's accounts, but it's as close to a clear picture as you're going to get.)

My phone rang and on the other end was a familiar voice letting me know it was one of my best friend's birthdays, and they were going to a concert in Denver to celebrate. With nothing but the spa outfit on my back (gray sweatpants and a YSL hoodie) I apparently ordered an Uber, headed to the airport, and woke up in Denver a few hours later. An interstate blackout takes a lot of practice, I assure you. Within an hour of landing, I'd taken a hit of acid, downed a few milk stouts, and promptly vomited. You can understand by this point, I'm sure, why my nickname in college was "Yackson."

The trip came to an end, and I poured myself back onto a flight home. LA was calling, and I had to go. Then, something unexpected happened. Things got better. Business improved, accounts placed orders, and suddenly it felt like I was getting into the swing of things. My days were filled with many of the same tasks familiar to anyone who works a corporate sales job. I went out on calls, helped fill orders, and generally assisted my then-boss with making sure our accounts were happy. We finally found our sweet spot when they started deploying me to stores in West Hollywood, or—as it's rightfully known on *30 Rock*—the People's Gaypublic of Drugifornia. In one particularly memorable instance, an ordering manager of a collective asked if I'd be interested in going to a circuit party. I quickly pulled out my phone and did a Google search for what that term meant—*oh my god, absolutely not.* "Sure! But how about placing an order with us?" To be clear, I've never attended a so-called circuit party.

From that point on, my drinking just got worse. But it didn't seem to matter, I was a *functioning* alcoholic. See, it's right there in the name, *functioning*. The leadership team from our headquarters in Colorado visited at least once a month to check up on us and make sure things were going smoothly. I've always loved to cook, so anytime we were "in the presence" (a term coined for being in the same room as the Queen, but appropriate here), I'd always whip up an elaborate dinner. On this trip, the entrée du jour was chicken parm, a staple in my home. We sat around the dining room table, sharing war stories about the California market, and counting our victories along with our losses. If Colorado had been the great experiment, California was the great test of patience. The reality was, we'd been given an impossible task. Looking back, it's actually sort of an honor—everyone knew it probably wouldn't work, but they thought that we were the best equipped to try.

It was becoming increasingly apparent that I just wasn't cut out to be part of a sales team. I found the interactions with store managers to be frustrating, and seeing sales roll in just didn't excite me. It was a time of conflict in my own life, an era of professional failing, mixed with what would later turn out to be personal growth. The company had signed on to sponsor a cross-country tour for a well-known band, and I'd been tasked with handling some of the marketing efforts for the event. Though daunting at first, I found the work rewarding. It involved dealing with decision makers and convincing them why working with us was a good idea. It wasn't so much about buying our products as it was about buying our *vision*. I worked to make a compelling argument on behalf of the brand about why aligning with the company offered some sort of reputational advancement. It was my first taste of really putting my college education to use, and it started to feel like I was on the right path again.

In the end, California wasn't for me. I missed my friends and was in the throes of a family health crisis back in Colorado. Quietly, I started to build a case for why returning to Colorado would make sense for the company. It was just like any other Tuesday—our team was conducting a pop-up at a collective, plying consumers with promo items and schmoozing with sales managers to carry more of our products. My phone beeped, and I made my way out to the car. I'd scheduled some time to speak with the owners about a new idea: what if I came back to Colorado and instead of struggling to make it in a sales role, put my skills to work and ran our company's social media? The call started at its schedule time, and I dove headfirst into a well-executed verbal PowerPoint about the merits of having someone like me run our social strategy. It was filled with cringe-worthy corporate buzzwords like synergy, metrics, and robust data collection. I suppose maybe I had learned *something* from sales after all, and my case was convincing enough that I got the green light to head back home.

I broke the news to my roommates that I'd be ditching them for greener pastures. I wish I could say that I regretted leaving them in the lurch, but I don't. Leaving California was the best thing I'd done in ages, and I instantly felt a huge sense of relief, though it may have just been the handful of Xanax I'd taken a few minutes prior. I'm not sure that I had second thoughts about leaving, but my decision was made concrete when I arranged to have my car shipped back to Colorado. The car shipper who showed up at my door could only be described as a caricature of a Russian mobster. With slicked-back blond hair and a studded leather jacket—*in California....in the summer*—he asked for my keys and took a look at the car. I'd compiled a pretty healthy stockpile of all manner of edibles from the collectives in California and wasn't prepared to let them go to waste. I stuffed them in every crevice of any suitcase I could find and loaded them into the car. My X5 smelled like a Migos concert. The Russian mobster-car-shipping-expert popped open the doors, took a sniff, and looked me dead in the eyes. *Oh shit, the jig is up*, I thought. "Two hundred dollar extra fee for luggage," he shouted in a thick accent. I opted against paying and lugged a few suitcases out of the car, vowing to eat every last edible rather than fork over an additional $200.

For me, California had proven to be a failure. I'd succumbed to homesickness, fallen deeper into my own personal battle with drugs and alcohol, and generally felt a sense that I'd let people down. The silver lining was getting closer to finally narrowing down what exactly it was I wanted to do. Working in cannabis had been both exciting and new, but I yearned to find a way to make it fit into my life in a way that meant more. One of the owners of the company offers a simple guideline for being successful at our organization: bring value. I knew that if I were going to return to Colorado, I had only one task—prove my value in the larger scheme of our business. If being on the West Coast had taught me anything, it's that there's more to life than watching Bravo and chugging white wine.

Working in social media felt like a step in the right direction. I'd always had a penchant for selling stories to people, and it struck me that posting pictures on a corporate Facebook page was simply the electronic version of that skill. What if, after all this, I wasn't destined to shill products in a store, but rather to use my own network to sell the *idea* of our products. At the time, it was all too abstract, and a bit too far out of reach. I said my farewells and headed to LAX (I feel obligated to use this platform to point out that it is, in my opinion, the worst airport in America, and I pray that an industrial designer reads this and takes heed). I landed back in my home state, unlocked the door to my new apartment, and things felt like they might be looking up.

It would be a cliché to call it the calm before the storm, but dear god, there was a storm brewing.

INTERVIEW WITH JOHN MOYNAN

John Moynan, twenty-nine, is the general counsel for Organa Brands. A graduate of Arizona State University and Colorado Law, he's one of the youngest GC's in the country. He assumed the role in 2017 and has negotiated hundreds of cannabis contracts and licensing deals, all valued in the high eight figures. The law and the cannabis industry may at first seem like they'd be at odds, so I spoke to John to find out why that might not quite be the case.

What's it like being the general counsel for one of the largest cannabis companies in the country? What does your typical day look like?

·I feel incredibly fortunate. I've spent the entirety of my professional career at the same company, so it's easy to get lost in the day-to-day and normalize the abnormal, but we really are so fortunate to be working in an industry that is so dynamic and offers so much opportunity. There's no way my career path (and the career paths of many of the people around me) would have been possible in any other industry at any other time.

It's hard to really describe a typical day. Atypical is the norm around here, which is why I love my job so much.

What's the most misunderstood aspect of cannabis laws?

I think most people expect that, once you get past the whole federal illegality issue, there is some sort of consistency amongst the state laws, which couldn't be further from the truth. There's really not a cohesive set of rules or laws that governs how a business operates on a national level, which forces cannabis companies to either become hyper-localized or completely re-envision the ways in which they do business.

Did you ever expect this is what you'd be doing for a living? More to the point, were you a D.A.R.E. kid?

Definitely not. I grew up in a fairly conservative household that was fairly close-minded when it came to cannabis. I'm not sure if I met all the qualifications to be considered a D.A.R.E kid, but I definitely owned the T-shirt at one point. I participated in the industry as a consumer through most of college, and the opportunity to participate in this space was mostly a byproduct of circumstance rather than an intentional decision. Since joining Organa Brands, I've developed a real appreciation for cannabis, and the once-closed-minded family has come around as well. I really couldn't have asked for a more ideal career in a more ideal industry.

On a scale from "patchwork" to "clusterfuck," how would you describe the interaction of federal, state, and local cannabis laws?

"Clusterfuck" may be my single-most used word over the last five years here. Nothing is ever easy in this industry, and that certainly includes navigating the legal landscape. Each state has its own entirely unique set of regulations by which we are required to abide, and each local municipality adds another layer to that complexity. Navigating a dozen plus (only including the markets we're currently in) complex legal frameworks would be difficult enough on its own. Add in the fact that each of these are constantly, dramatically changing as the industry develops, and it creates a massive clusterfuck.

How does it compare to Canada? What are the pros and cons of each market's unique regulations?

Canada is ahead of the game in a lot of respects, but is still very much figuring things out for itself. The biggest difference is obviously the federal legality, and the impact that has on taking on institutional investment, finding access to public markets, and working with established vendors, firms, etc. Outside of that, they are actually a bit behind several states in many respects in my opinion.

What do you think will need to be accomplished in order to see federal legalization in the United States?

It's going to take an act of Congress, and we all know how effective that branch of government has been over the last decade in particular. You'd think that it's an issue that both parties could work into their platforms. It's as easy to cast it as a civil rights issue as it is to cast it as a states rights issue. That being said, I won't be holding my breath waiting for Congress to pull it together and accomplish something meaningful.

Think of a specific moment in time when you realized you were working in uncharted territory. Have you ever had doubts about working in this space?

I remember drafting a supply agreement very early in my career, and I was pulling templates from one of the legal document repositories we use. I was complaining to the attorney I was working for at the time about how none of the templates would really work in the regulatory environment we were operating in. He said something along the lines of "Well, yeah, I can't imagine one of these has ever been drafted for cannabis before, and certainly not at this scale." It was crazy to think that such a small document could still be so unprecedented in this context. I was, and am, super grateful to be a part of that growth.

What complexities does the cannabis space face that other "vice" industries do not?

I think the biggest complexity relates to the fact that it is all ever-changing. The whole industry is still trying to figure itself out, so whether you're talking legally, or in any other area of our business, every decision made is an attempt to hit a moving target.

CHAPTER 4

Taxes!
(Please keep reading.)

It's imperative to understand some of the complexities surrounding the world of marijuana, though perhaps not those that would first come to mind. Thus far, when talking about a regulated cannabis market, we haven't been discussing greed or politics—or even drugs, for that matter—though it can, and often does, involve plenty of those things. When we discuss the cannabis industry, what we're really talking about are the humanistic qualities of the individuals who constitute its existence. It's a story about a few unlikely characters whose lives would unexpectedly collide and forever alter the history of an emerging industry.

In this instance, it's a story of a senator from an oft-overlooked state, a president who segued from Hollywood to politics, and a peddler of intoxicants just trying to make a living. These three narratives would converge, resulting in a complex system of tax laws that would later act as a massive barrier for those within the regulated cannabis industry for years to come. Though our story begins some forty years ago, the effect of their actions are still very much alive in 2019.

Born in 1923 in an unremarkable home on North Maple Drive in Russell, Kansas, Bob Dole represents the quintessential American success story. (Yes, that Bob Dole. I can feel you tuning out already. Stay with me.) The son of a dairy farmer, he excelled in sports from a young age, and later played basketball, football, and ran track at the University of Kansas. His mother, Bina, sold Singer sewing machines door-to-door. Salesmanship was clearly a part of the Dole DNA, which might perhaps explain why Bob would go on to pedal Viagra on television some fifty years later, as a paid spokesperson for Pfizer. Always congenial and a true people-person, he was named Man of the Year by his brothers in Kappa Sigma fraternity. As is the case with many political careers in his generation, World War II interrupted his education and he enlisted in the Army. After leaving the service, Dole used the G.I. Bill to enroll in college, where he earned both an undergraduate degree and a JD. His political aspirations began shortly after graduation, when he was elected to the House of Representatives, where he held a seat from 1961–1969. He was then elected to the Senate, serving from 1969 through 1996, when he left the Senate and became the Republican presidential nominee for president, ultimately losing to Bill Clinton.

In the early days of Dole's Senate career, while he was shaping political sentiment across the country, another man found himself changing the direction of US politics for decades to come too—only he didn't realize it. Jeffrey Edmondson was a burgeoning entrepreneur. His sales territory was immense, his clients diverse. Upon seeing a gap in the market, Edmondson swooped down from the vast metropolis that is the Twin Cities and made his debut on the business landscape. His first few years were unremarkable, but he later carved out a niche for himself that proved to be not only lucrative, but exciting. A true capitalist, he made a living by meeting the needs of others. His business was one of countless others in an industry that had existed for generations, sometimes as family-run operations, sometimes one-man shows. Edmondson was a drug dealer. Not the head of a cartel or the mob, just a mid-level guy from the suburbs of Minneapolis. He bought cocaine by the ounce, marijuana by the pound, and pills by the million.

In 1981, after being charged with drug-related crimes and serving a seven-year sentence, Edmondson found himself the subject of an IRS investigation over failure to report income. The IRS wanted its share of the income he'd made selling narcotics. According to court records, "his primary source of controlled substances was one Jerome Caby, who delivered the goods to petitioner in Minneapolis on consignment. Petitioner paid Caby after the drugs were sold." My thanks to the IRS for explaining to us the definition of "consignment." As drug dealers do, Edmondson traveled extensively, sometimes as far west as San Diego, to sell amphetamines and cocaine to the masses. According to court records, he drove twenty-nine thousand miles in the taxable year 1974 alone. Where *did* he find the energy?

Like any respectable criminal, Edmondson sought to reduce his tax obligation to the IRS by submitting his expenses. Selling drugs is hard work, I assure you. An evident high-roller during business trips, in 1974 (just one of several years of failed reporting under investigation), he spent $200 on airfare, $250 on food and entertainment, and $180 on long-distance phone calls. (For readers under the age of twenty-five, a long-distance call originated from a different area code than the number being dialed, resulting in an itemized charge on the month-end bill. Please ask your grandparents for further detail, and be sure to reference BellSouth's then-generous calling plan for added color.)

The IRS challenged his ability to deduct expenses, but Edmondson sued the IRS and won. The court found that the expenses he incurred from his illegal drug business were, indeed, legal. This was thanks in large part to the Cohan rule, which allows reasonable estimates to be used for expenses when actual records cannot be produced. In 1981's Edmondson v. Commissioner, the court found that even though Edmondson didn't keep records, "claimed business expenses consist of the purchase of a small scale, packaging expenses, telephone expenses, and automobile expenses...were made in connection with petitioner's trade or business and were both ordinary and necessary." That must have stung.

In total, Mr. Edmondson claimed $106,000 for his cost of goods sold and tried to write off reasonable business expenses as part of the investigation. His expenses were originally disallowed but the court found that his "role in the drug market, together with his appearance and candor at trial, cause us to believe that he was honest, forthright, and candid in his reconstruction of the income and expenses from his illegal activities." Under the oversight of the court, Edmondson led a hallmark challenge against the IRS in order to deduct his expenses related to illegal activities from his tax liability. Can we take a moment to imagine what that scene must have looked like? I picture a street dealer sitting in a conference room, listing out, from memory, all of the dime bags and pills he'd sold over the year prior. "Well, there was the pound of Northern Lights I bought in January along with an ounce of coke, then in February I purchased a thousand pills..." An honest and precise dealer, a rare breed to be sure.

Prior to this moment, the federal tax code had never contemplated a drug dealer loophole. That was all about to change. This is the moment where the lives of our two characters, a drug dealer and a politician, are about to converge. The effects wouldn't be realized for many years, but they would send a ripple across an industry that wasn't yet in its infancy. So severe was the impact that, decades later, the regulated cannabis industry would find itself being treated as an illegitimate business despite state legislation making it legal. The now-closed "Edmondson Loophole" would prove a pain point for anyone contemplating entering the world of legal cannabis.

A year later, Dole was still nursing his wounds from a failed attempt to win a spot in the White House as the Republican vice presidential nominee running alongside Gerald Ford. While he hadn't made it to the White House, he did find himself climbing the ranks of the Senate. He was serving as chair of the Senate Finance Committee, when an obscure case from the US tax court came across his desk. Bob Dole didn't like drug dealers. Bob Dole didn't like people who cheated the system. Bob Dole didn't much care for young whippersnappers making a mockery of the law. What Bob Dole did like was Bob Dole. He had long possessed a penchant for referring to himself in the third person, a trait that, by my own assessment, can only be attributed to someone with a deep love of self. Always clad in a navy suit and a patterned tie, the regalia of any true conservative, he was a stern man with little time for nonsense. The war many years prior had hardened him, and his role in the Finance Committee had sharpened his focus on enhancing the financial and, by extension, reputational standing of the United States. With Ronald Reagan in the White House, the public's attention had turned its focus to controlled substances, and the War on Drugs was in full swing.

Seeing an opportunity to make a political statement masquerading as finance reform, Rep. Fortney Pete Stark (D-CA-9) seized on the opportunity to introduce TEFRA, also known as the Tax Equity and Fiscal Responsibility Act of 1982. The bill was soon taken from the House to a Senate committee chaired by Bob Dole. What better way to hinder a developing market than drowning it in tax burdens?

Bob Dole, like many politicians, was not working alone. In the time leading up to the passage of TEFRA, a first-term Republican senator named William "Bill" Armstrong sponsored an amendment to the bill. Armstrong was a devout Christian, known for his lifelong (and very creative) catchphrase "Jesus, Jesus, Jesus." I'm not totally clear what that expression meant to him, but I must admit I've shouted the same words at cars who cut me off on the 405. His amendment, as you probably guessed, was Section 280E. Written deep within TEFRA were a few seemingly innocuous lines:

"No deduction or credit shall be allowed for any amount paid or incurred during the taxable year in carrying on any trade or business

41

if such trade or business (or the activities which comprise such trade or business) consists of trafficking in controlled substances (within the meaning of schedule I and II of the Controlled Substances Act) which is prohibited by Federal law or the law of any State in which such trade or business is conducted."

President Reagan signed the bill into law and, without knowing it, forever altered the landscape in which a regulated cannabis market would exist many decades later. Let's take a moment to appreciate the supreme irony of the fact that a senator from Colorado, the perfect example of responsible cannabis reform, would add an amendment to a bill that would cripple its most lucrative industry almost three decades later. In 2017, another Republican senator from Colorado, one Cory Gardner, was poised to take on 280E and defend the cannabis industry from the IRS.

"Our current tax code puts thousands of legal marijuana businesses throughout Colorado at a disadvantage by treating them differently than other businesses across the state," Gardner said in an interview with the *Denver Post* in 2017. "Coloradans made their voices heard in 2012 when they legalized marijuana, and it's time for the federal government to allow Colorado businesses to compete. This commonsense, bipartisan bill will allow small businesses in Colorado and other states that have legal marijuana businesses to grow their operations, create jobs, and boost the economy."

Gardner is something of an enigma. He opposed same-sex marriage in 2010, and as recently as 2018 voted to ban abortions after twenty weeks. For many, his more liberal stance on cannabis was something of a surprise—until we consider the sheer amount of cannabis dollars that flow through his home state. The implication, of course, is that gay marriage and abortion don't create jobs in Colorado, or at least, none that compete with the scale of the cannabis industry. The Small Business Tax Equity Act of 2017, which Gardner co-sponsored, came as somewhat of a shock to those who have followed his politics. In part, the bill seeks to reform 280E and allow cannabis businesses to flourish in much the same fashion as their intoxicant counterparts, Coors and Einstein Bros. Bagels, which are also headquartered in the state. (Okay, maybe bagels don't qualify as an intoxicant to everyone, but try getting sober and let me know what your carb intake looks like. Some crave a frosty beer at the end of the day; I look forward to a scooped raisin bagel, toasted, with peanut butter, thank you very much.)

Back to the point. Much like his 1970s counterpart Armstrong, Gardner seeks to alter the economic landscape of his home state with just a few simple words. If he succeeds in adding one sentence to Section 280E, "unless such trade or business consists of marijuana sales conducted in compliance with State law," Mr. Gardner will forever change how cannabis businesses operate across the country.

In 2019, costs are high. Expectations are high. People are high. It's the cannabis industry after all, and for as much money is made, even more is given away. Many businesses in the space have a realized tax rate upwards of 100 percent. Imagine, for a moment, trying to launch a business with such a staggering tax rate. It's no wonder that many in the business take such issue with Section 280E. Creating a business is hard work, creating a successful one even more so. Despite the seeming popularity of the cannabis industry in the United States, there's never been a worse time to get started. The market is seeing an unparalleled compression of wholesale costs, as consolidation takes place across verticals. Consolidation has proven to be a general theme across the industry, particularly in the last three years, as more and more companies merge, many of them with the goal of listing on a public exchange. There's a huge push toward a shared services model, where companies can pool resources to reduce costs and expand their distribution efforts by partnering with complementary assets. In the case of our company, Organa Brands merged with its Canadian parent company, SLANG Worldwide, in addition to two other cannabis businesses. As time goes on, the well-established legacy businesses gain momentum until they are well funded enough to buy out their competition. So too is the case in the cannabis world, where dispensaries are bought out by larger chains, distributors swallow up brands to add to their pipelines, and grow facilities merge with larger ones more equipped to handle production. Add all of this to the complex issues arising from the federal tax code, and we have something of a mess on our hands.

Despite the many obstacles they face, cannabis industrialists have proven time and again that they won't be slowed by government interference. In fact, many have seen the complexities as an arbitrage opportunity. The rise of tax specialists and corporate structure consultants who focus on cannabis have seen a boom alongside the core business of the industry itself. The search for tax loopholes is as American as apple pie and fireworks on the Fourth of July. I reiterate this point time and again—cannabis businesses are just like any others. Sure, they exist in an often-complex patchwork of state-by-state regulations, but they follow the same key business tenets as any other consumer goods companies. Intellectual property is created, products are manufactured, and the resulting goods marketed and advertised. They're then sold to consumers via new or existing retail channels, and the resulting profits go back into the business. Without the undue burden laid upon the industry by the IRS, we'd see cannabis businesses unshackle themselves from years of unfair taxation and emerge as a formidable opponent in the global business arena. Social causes aside, America is a country that's built on capitalism. It's the promise of a better life through hard work and monetary gain. If we're to collectively raise the state of our nation to its highest levels, we must first ask ourselves why we punish some vices more than others. A blossoming cannabis industry will create hundreds of thousands of jobs, add billions of dollars to the economy, and create a lasting revenue stream for future generations.

What does it mean for a business to not be able to itemize and deduct its expenses from its tax liability? Let's imagine, for a moment, that you wanted to open an escort service. Escort services, often lumped in with similar vice industries, are treated as normal businesses, despite some small measure of additional regulation and oversight. A prospective escort company would need to go through all the usual motions to get up and running. They'd choose a name, let's call it Definitely Not a Brothel LLC. Definitely Not a Brothel would file articles of incorporation with the secretary of state wherever they want to operate. They'd keep a receipt of the state fees incurred while registering, as well as receipts for any expenses relating to attorney or accounting fees. Definitely Not a Brothel LLC could even incorporate in Delaware, as 65 percent of publicly traded US companies choose to do. Once the business is properly licensed, the owner would go ahead and get started on the nuts and bolts. They'd sign a lease on their new office, buy paper and office supplies, and set up a 401(k) contribution program for their employees. Because they aren't a cannabis company, all of these expenses qualify as reasonable and necessary, and could thus be deducted from their tax liability.

Let's imagine that Definitely Not a Brothel LLC began to gain some traction. Suddenly, their workforce expanded, and new operational costs popped up faster than one of their more senior clients who'd just taken a little blue pill. On the advice of a tax accountant, they discover that almost every one of their daily expenses is deductible. Operational expenses, such as flights, meals, home offices, and mileage, plus payroll, rent, and insurance costs can all be written off. Hell, they can even write off hair extensions and high heels, so long as they can provide a receipt and an explanation for their necessity in a business transaction. Anyone who owns a business sings the praises of the itemized deduction section of their tax forms come April 15. Any business, so long as they aren't selling a scheduled substance, can itemize their business expenses and thus reduce their tax liability, freeing up extra capital to grow. Cannabis, unlike its other vice-industry counterparts, enjoys no commonality with similarly regulated industries, thanks in large part to 280E and its inclusion on the DEA's list of scheduled substances.

One can look no further than the pharmaceutical industry to see the inequality inherent in 280E. In 2015, American taxpayers subsidized more than $6 billion in advertising expenses from pharmaceutical companies. Advertising costs are exempted expenses and can be written off when filing taxes. To understand how unusual this is, we have to first realize that the United States is one of only two countries to permit advertising for pharmaceuticals. More Americans died from prescription drug overdoses in 2016 than died in the entirety of the Vietnam war, according to CDC data and a recent piece in the *New York Times*. Why did cannabis, a substance that has never once directly caused an overdose, come to be so severely punished by the federal tax code?

When I was a teenager, I always had a fairly good sense of what was a good idea and what was a bad one. That is, from an early age, I was able to trust my internal compass to tell me right from wrong. I'm sure a great deal of that was attributable to my parents and grandmother, who seemingly without effort raised an odd, precocious, and flamboyant young man. I did well in school, made friends easily, and overall, had a happy upbringing. I tell you all of this to brace you for a short tale of youthful idiocy. We'd recently moved into a new home, a cookie-cutter replica of the house one block down the road. It was suburban living at its finest, and a far departure from the 110-year-old Victorian house we'd lived in for the decade prior. It was a typical winter night in Colorado, blizzard coming down, and my parents had flipped the wall switch to ignite a blaze inside our new, glass-front fireplace. I was fourteen years old and had, at most, a pseudo-understanding of the laws of physics. Clearly in dire need of some type of stupidity exorcism, I went out to the backyard and made a snowball. When I came back proudly into the living room, tiny snowflakes were clinging to my brow. The glass front of the fireplace was scalding, having been slowly licked by flames for the better part of an evening. My parents were watching reruns of the *Daily Show with Jon Stewart* (my ninety-one-year-old grandmother's ultimate celebrity crush...I get it). In one swift motion, I hurled the snowball at the fireplace. POP! It sounded like someone had just fired a starting pistol directly into my eardrum. You can imagine what happened—a scalding piece of untempered glass met with a freezing cold lump of snow. The snowball hit with such force that I startled even myself. I'm fairly confident that was the first—and last—time I'd ever thrown a ball (or participated in anything that could be construed as a sport, for that matter). The glass exploded, sending tiny shards flying through the living room like a Gulfstream through Cayman airspace. My parents were stunned. They'd thought they had raised a smart kid. Why did we pay for these good schools, I'm sure they wondered, if we're just going to end up with a kid who doesn't know freezing cold and burning hot don't mix?

Like that fireplace, the cannabis industry is hot. It's been retaining raw energy for the last three decades. The glass wall that makes up its public image is blistering, threatening to singe the knuckle hair off of anyone who dares to approach it. With 280E, the IRS made a snowball. Sure, they had made them before. It's the See What Sticks method. They toss them at passersby and see what makes an impact. Usually, thanks to bureaucratic bloat that makes my post-Thanksgiving body look like a Sports Illustrated model, the snowballs, or in this case the regulations, fail to stick. They crumple under their own weight and fall apart before ever becoming airborne. The spring sun emerges on April 15, the snow melts, and most forget about the IRS until the following winter. Not so with 280E. It's a constant reminder that businesses like ours are not viewed as normal or legitimate. This small line of text in the federal tax code is more like permafrost than snow, unrelenting, bitter cold, and poised to shatter the white-hot glass that the IRS has launched it toward. I suspect that much like my youthful act of stupidity and its absence of foresight, the original framers of this provision of the tax code never imagined a regulated cannabis industry. Indeed, I doubt they realized the impact these few lines of text would have on a future multi-billion dollar sector. 280E is out to shatter an industry.

Remember when I mentioned that cannabis businesses can pay an effective tax rate as high as 100 percent? It should now begin to make a little more sense how that's possible. 280E has emerged as a pair of hands gripping the neck of cannabis businesses across the country. It's squeezing every last dime out of their pockets and making meaningful expansion virtually impossible for many. Without the ability to deduct expenses, these businesses are paying more in taxes than those in practically any other sector in the world. In a 2018 study, the analytics firm New Frontier Data found that "combining the business tax revenues, the payroll withholdings based on the theoretical employment required to support the industry, and the 15 percent retail sales tax, one can calculate the total federal tax revenue potential of legalization: The combined total is estimated to be $105.6 billion." Almost $106 billion in federal tax revenue, simply by legalizing cannabis. If the IRS thought they'd hit the jackpot with 280E, they clearly haven't contemplated the increased tax revenue that would be brought about by federal legalization. For an added layer of context, the three largest oil and gas providers in the US, ConocoPhillips, Chevron, and Exxon Mobil paid a combined $289 billion in taxes between 2007–2012. The cannabis industry could provide almost half the amount of federal tax revenue as three of the most powerful companies in America.

To understand the true impact of measures like 280E, we have to better understand their intent. The Senate report that was issued alongside 280E makes it crystal clear:

There is a sharply defined public policy against drug dealing. To allow drug dealers the benefit of business expense deductions at the same time that the US and its citizens are losing billions of dollars per year to such persons is not compelled by the fact that such deductions are allowed to other, legal, enterprises. Such deductions must be disallowed on public policy grounds.

At face value, the excerpt makes sense. There's no reason that drug dealers, participating in an illegal business, should be entitled to the same benefits as their legitimate counterparts. The issue here is that the writers of TEFRA, and by extension 280E, never contemplated a market in which regulated cannabis businesses could legally exist. I'm sure it seemed as far-fetched as an alleged sexual predator-turned-reality game show host being elected president. Well, strange things have been happening in American history—cannabis is legal in thirty-three states, and Donald Trump rules over them as president. Even with the help of Allison DuBois, I doubt Bob Dole and Bill Armstrong would've been able to predict that turn of events. But alas, just like the president's orange hue, the cannabis industry is here to stay (though not without the help of some seriously high-powered bulbs).

CHAPTER 5

Little Black Dots *or* How I Learned to Stop Worrying and Love Triple-Overtime

I'd fled California with my tail between my legs. I'd failed at my new job as a brand ambassador and had a rocky relationship with my now-former roommates. None of it mattered to me. It may have been the Xanax, but I was just relieved to be returning to Colorado and my old friends. Relief washed over me the moment I stepped off the plane in Denver. After managing to convince the owners of the company that I should take on a new role as social media manager, it felt like things might be looking up, and I could have a new purpose with which to distract myself from the drug dependency that was creeping more steadily into my daily life.

The company had hired a marketing consultant, and I was to report directly to him. It was a strange change of pace. The consultant arrived straight from corporate America and didn't have the time or the interest to participate in anything relating to cannabis, or workplace, culture. He arrived on time each day and left the moment the clock struck five. It wasn't a bad rhythm, just not one to which I had grown accustomed. I'd taken several social media classes in college, so I thought myself something of an expert on the subject, a belief that would soon be shattered as the reality and complexities of cannabis social media settled in.

Coming from my apartment a few blocks from the office, the daily struggle of medication management started to play a distinct role in my work output. I'd begin each day by reaching for a bottle of Ritalin—Daddy's little helpers. I'd head into the kitchen and grab a glass of water, take a pill out of the bottle, and reconsider my decision. Thirty seconds later, I'd be crushing the pill beneath an expired credit card, snorting the fine white powder, and chugging a glass of water to soothe the burning post-nasal drip that followed the rush of inhaling my medication. "Use as directed" always seemed a little vague.

The company was expanding rapidly, and we needed a social media program that could both keep pace with the industry and maneuver through the complexities of online advertising in the world of regulated cannabis. The company had built a solid following in the year prior to my taking on this new role, but I'd been determined to get up to speed and keep the growth moving. For someone obsessed with keeping up with the Joneses both online and off, social media felt like the perfect outlet for the creative interests I'd largely been ignoring. It was a chance to take a message, massage it, and spin it out to the masses online. It was my first taste of public relations and I was hooked. Social media, however, would prove to be an exercise in biting off more than I could chew.

In the cannabis world, it's important to note how vastly different the rules of social media are applied. Across the board, cannabis brands are generally banned from social media platforms, as their mere existence violates most terms and conditions. Take Instagram for example, whose terms and conditions state "Offering sexual services, buying or selling firearms and illegal or prescription drugs *(even if it's legal in your region)* is also not allowed." While the terms don't specifically list cannabis as banned content, they effectively give the platform free rein to shut down such accounts. Cannabis, in the eyes of most social platforms, is an illegal drug. Any account that promotes the sale or use of drugs, legal or not, has no standing to defend account deletion on Facebook, Twitter, or Instagram. In practice, the ramifications are much more severe. Sponsored content, otherwise known as paid social ads, are the backbone of any business competing online today. Like countless other advertising channels, cannabis businesses are barred from running paid ads on most social media platforms, essentially eliminating any possibility of growing a platform through paid ads and sponsored content. It should come as no surprise at this point that because of intense regulations from mainstream social media platforms, many thought it a good idea to start social networking tools that not only allowed cannabis, but whose very existence was rooted in cannabis itself. Apps like Duby offer a cannabis-centric take on the modern social network.

It's unclear when these policies might change, but they are far from an aberration. Take traditional advertising channels as an example: billboards, TV spots, radio placements, and online banner ads. Each comes with its own unique set of rules that vary state by state. Not so long ago, we went to purchase an electronic billboard during a cannabis conference in a major city. The artwork was submitted, the invoice was paid, and we assumed we were good to go. Then the phone rang with my advertising broker calling to let me know they'd received a memo from the city informing them that they would be fined if cannabis ads were allowed to run. Alcohol ads run freely on billboards across America. Cannabis ads, however, have proven to be too tough a pill to swallow for many regulators. With cannabis legal in some form in thirty-three states, I have to wonder at what point will we get our share of the advertising arena.

Perhaps the most complex aspect of advertising lies in the patchwork of varying cannabis laws that form the map of regulated states. In Colorado, for example, no cannabis brand can be advertised on a platform in which a person could reasonably expect more than 30 percent of the potential viewers would be under the age of twenty-one. And that's just one state. Now multiply that by thirty-three, plus the individual municipalities that make up each location, and you can begin to understand why cannabis advertising is something of a black box.

My foray into social media management turned into a job that, at the time, was almost impossible to succeed in. The restrictions were so tightly enforced, it was extremely difficult to engage with a large audience. We tried everything—cannabis cooking recipes, contests, even the lowest form of social media, girls in bikinis. The latter, my harebrained idea, was one of my more poorly thought out concepts. I'd decided to post some photos from a pool party we'd sponsored where several girls in branded bikinis posed in front of our custom-wrapped VW bus. The reception was lukewarm, save for one particularly damning email that arrived in my inbox. It was from the leader of a local women's coalition, who had deemed me not just a misogynist, but a woman-hating, heteronormative example of what was wrong with men in America. I've been called a lot of things. But heteronormative? That's not an insult this Beyoncé-loving, crop top-wearing, fashion-advice-giving gay can stomach. I typed an email that should've started "Listen, honey," but instead started "To whom it may concern." I explained my decision-making process, offered an apology, and vowed for the second time in my life to never look at, or even think of, a woman in a bikini again.

My workload was once again grueling, as the company continued to expand, adding Connecticut to our list of operations. We had hit a sales record in Colorado, and business was booming. In cannabis culture, there's a special day—an event like no other. It's Christmas for Chronic, Hanukkah for Hash, and Kwanza for Kush:

April 20, otherwise known as 4/20. There are all sorts of urban legends about how 4/20 first came to be. They range from the police code for "smoking cannabis in progress" being listed as code 420, to a story about an assembly date for fans of the Grateful Dead. The real story, however, originates in a San Rafael, California, high school in the early 1970s, where three students, "The Waldos," had established a time to meet near a statue in front of their school to begin a hunt for a long lost marijuana crop. They met each day at the same time, and although they never found the weed, they left a lasting mark on cannabis culture. It wasn't until some years later that *High Times* Editor Steve Hager began using the phrase in association with cannabis meetups, and thus 4/20 entered the zeitgeist.

It was early February 2015, and the 4/20 planning had begun. We'd decided to unveil a new product, a vaporizer cartridge filled with pure, high-potency cannabis oil. After weeks of searching for a name, we'd landed on *Reserve*, and the R&D team began working with the marketing department to get a launch plan into place. Packaging was ordered, ads were designed, and marketing collateral—posters, postcards, and informational one-sheets—were printed. The sales team was instructed to commence with presales, and right out of the gate, the product was a huge success. It wasn't even on the market yet, and dispensaries were beating down our door to place orders. It became apparent that we might not be able to keep up with demand, thanks in large part to the product's complex packaging. We'd commissioned the Denver-based design firm EBD to create cutting-edge packaging, and they delivered. It was octagonal, with matte black finish, and constructed entirely out of recycled paper. To open it, the consumer would simply pull up on the package, causing it to bloom like a flower in the spring. (Internally, some nicknamed it the sphincter, but that's neither here nor there). It was, in a word, beautiful. Inside each package was a cartridge filled with the finest cannabis oil available on the market, adorned with a hand-tied hang tag on which we'd heat-embossed the relevant branding and product information. Oh, and did I mention that the whole package was created entirely using wind power? We're the hippies your parents warned you about.

Needless to say, the final product required an incredible amount of work to assemble. With 4/20 creeping closer and orders piling up in Salesforce, something had to give. The owners hatched a plan—if we wanted, employees could earn triple overtime for visiting the lab after work and helping with the assembly process. I'd had my eye on a new fur coat (remember what I said about constantly aligning with the stereotype of housewife?) so I happily obliged. When I arrived at the lab, it looked and felt more like a Russian bathhouse, thanks to all the bodies working tirelessly to fill orders. We were still a startup at this point, so the "all hands on deck" approach was common. Organa Labs, the facility in which the extraction took place, is the oldest licensed cannabis facility in America. If there were a national historical monument designation for cannabis extraction labs, this one would have a plaque on its front steps.

It was just another moment in a long line of occurrences that really drove home the notion that we weren't working at a normal company. As I looked around the lab, I noticed that every owner of the company was present, constructing boxes and gluing magnets onto hang-tags, alongside almost every employee from each rung of the company. Someone in the lab had a penchant for '80s music and had ordered in several loudspeakers from which to blare their favorite songs. It was hard not to to be motivated when the energy in the room was so palpable, though I guess it could have been the Ritalin I'd taken as well. Once again, I felt like I was part of some moment in history that we'd look back on and laugh at—working late nights for the simple, common goal of getting people high on amazing cannabis oil, during the annual celebration of its very existence. With "Come on Eileen" and "Thriller" blasting in the background, we worked late into the night for two weeks.

I've always had an issue with sweating—sweaty palms, sweaty feet, sweaty underarms. Remember that sweat problem I discussed earlier? Well, sweat and paper products don't mix, so while working in our steam room of a lab, I was forced to don black latex gloves to keep myself from dripping all over the goods. Eventually the gloves would fill, so I'd sport a lululemon sweatshirt with thumb cut-outs, originally designed for yoga poses, but it worked in a pinch to keep my sweat at bay. I only mention this to demonstrate the point that collectively we'd go to any lengths to get the job done.

Every day followed much the same pattern. I'd show up to the office at eight in the morning, work until five, and then head straight for the lab where music and catering would be waiting (though, I didn't do much eating, see also: Ritalin side effects). Eventually, we made a dent in the orders and started to feel like we were in a good place. One night, we noticed that there was a large box of hang-tags, around 5,000 or so, that still needed holes punched in the tops and elastic threads run through them. Alongside one of my best friends from college, Brittany, who also happened to be a colleague at this point, I took the box home for us to continue our work. We arrived at my apartment, loaded a bowl, and played *Legally Blonde* on the flatscreen. We stayed there until 2 a.m., poking holes and threading strings, getting higher with each passing moment. I still sometimes find little paper dots stuck to the inside of my sofa and clothing some four years later.

As 4/20 approached in 2015, I was reminded of my first April 20 celebration five years prior. CU Boulder had always been a haven for those with a penchant for weed. It was the end of my freshman year, and our group of friends woke up at four in the morning to head to our designated smoke spot, dubbed "the yacht club" for no real reason aside from our love of all things nautical. It was a cold spring morning, and we bundled up to make the trek from our dorm to the venue. We arrived, loaded a bowl, promptly returned home and went to bed, trying to conserve as much energy for the annual celebration that would occur at precisely 4:20 p.m. on the Norlin Quad, a mainstay of Boulder's campus. Around two that afternoon, we commenced our revelries with a so-called "eighth-off" where teams of two race to see how quickly they can finish an eighth of an ounce of cannabis. Each team selected their own tool for consumption—mine opted for a bong. Some chose simple glass pipes, some had spent all day rolling joints and blunts, while others assembled something called a gravity bong. For the uninitiated, a gravity bong involves taking a gallon milk jug, cutting the bottom off, and poking a hole in the milk cap. Once completed, you fill a sink with water, place the jug into it, and load a bowl into the cap. While slowly pulling the haphazard contraption from the water, the suction causes it to fill with a milky white smoke. You pop the top off and inhale. It's essentially a bong for boy scouts—a solution for getting high when you'd also like to work with your hands.

We'd been given the day off from classes, and as we wrapped up our eighth race, started to make our way to the quad. Up to this point, on April 20, ten thousand people would gather in Boulder to simultaneously light up as the clock struck 4:20. The university absolutely detests the event and has done everything in its power to stop it. We'd received an email from the university's chancellor some days prior that pleaded: "As another April 20 approaches, we are faced with concerns from students, parents, alumni, Regents, and community members about a repeat of last year's 4/20 event, we hope that you will choose not to participate in unlawful activity that debases the reputation of your University and degree, and will encourage your fellow Buffs to act with pride and remember who they really are." Tough luck, pal. We'd recently been named America's number one party school by *Playboy*, so university officials were scrambling to distance themselves from that title. Of course, the party went on, and as we sat on the field, my group of friends smoked until we couldn't get any higher, then promptly went to bed.

Little did we know, that would be the last 4/20 event to ever take place on Boulder's campus. The following year, the school hatched a scheme that, well, stunk. In the week leading up to April 20, crews poured fish-based fertilizer over every grassy area on campus. The resulting odor was pungent enough to make your eyes water and smelled like the dumpsters behind an all-you-can-eat-sushi buffet in Reno. The tradition carries on, of course, though in a much more organized fashion, now filled with corporate sponsors and emcees overseeing the event. Such was the case when I attended the 4/20 cup in Denver in spring of 2015.

After months of prep work making packaging and assembling displays, 4/20 arrived, and like the weed that filled our cartridges, it was intense. We'd sponsored a bus service where customers could catch a ride to the event and were legally allowed to consume cannabis en route. The interior of the shuttle was reminiscent of an Equinox sauna, if you replaced steam with smoke, and men ogling one another with people of various ages and genders simply sharing a joint with one another. It was my first 4/20 working in the cannabis industry, and simply put, it was mind-boggling. The glazed eyes and pungent aroma was overpowering, but somehow it felt natural, like we were all destined to reach this moment in time. In lieu of bar crawls and brewery tours, tens of thousands of Coloradans and out-of-state visitors came together with one common goal: to get as high as possible. It wasn't dissimilar to the first 4/20 event I'd attended back in Boulder, although this one had a different feeling. It was well organized, fully in compliance with the law, and filled with *normal* people you'd expect to see shopping at a farmer's market on the weekend. Gone were the days of "drug rugs," the woven hemp smocks of yesteryear, instead replaced by parents and young people alike, all converging on a fairplex in south Denver to share in their common interest. In lieu of fish fertilizer and displeased university officials, the space was filled with police monitoring everyone's safety, while largely allowing everyone to do as they pleased. In the five years since I started college, so much had changed in Colorado. Marijuana had become legal for adult use, yes, but it was more than just a change in laws. Both the industry and the people who used its products had grown up. It was no longer just about getting high. It was about sharing in something great, some huge societal shift in which we no longer needed to be ashamed of partaking. We were not just allowed, but *encouraged* to celebrate the plant.

What caused this shift?

In the years since marijuana had become legal for adult use in Colorado, the sky hadn't fallen. In fact, there was increased evidence that legalization was working. Fewer people were in jail for petty marijuana possession, teen use had dropped, and a regulated market had begun to replace the black market. It was more than just the raw data that signaled the change—it was the shift in customers who came through the doors of the dispensaries. I'd spent an inordinate amount of time inside the four walls of pot shops throughout Colorado. In college, it was the same old crowd: Deadheads wearing tie-dye, college students skipping class, and a smattering of people from an older generation ducking their heads as they went in and out to conceal their identities.

By 2015, it had changed. The parking lots were now filled with minivans, while inside the store, moms stopped by and picked up vape pens instead of driving to the liquor store to grab bottles of moscato. In the blink of an eye, cannabis in Colorado had gone from a tool of the counterculture to just another intoxicant. Weed was so commonplace that people seemingly stopped caring who knew that they used it. More than anything else, it was a sign of what was to come in the rest of the country. If Colorado could not only try it, but succeed, who knew what was possible for other, less progressive states. And 4/20 wasn't just a day to get high, it was the physical embodiment of the social progression that had taken place in Colorado in just a few years. Cannabis was no longer a lifestyle. It was a tool for a better life. I had to wonder if we even needed social media to sell marijuana. From where I was standing, it appeared that weed might just be able to sell itself. Perhaps, it was more than just another consumer packaged good. The role of cannabis in society was shifting once again, and it was happening faster than anyone could have foreseen.

CHAPTER 6

It Starts with a Promise

This fucking sucks. During this particular time in my life, that phrase was my motto, my mantra, my *Real Housewives* tagline. I'd spent the better part of the previous twenty-four hours fighting with a varied assortment of friends and strangers about, as was customary by this point, nothing at all. My actions of the days prior were, like my internet search history, both shocking and primed for deletion. It was May 2, 2015, and I'd been living in Denver since January. My dad had suffered a traumatic brain injury in 2014, so it seemed like I should try to put my drink down and spend a bit of quality time with the people who'd dedicated the bulk of their adult lives to me. Only one of those things happened, however, and I instead spent my time in Colorado taking full advantage of having ready access to my old general practitioner and the cornucopia of prescription pills that came along with her. Coupled with a fixation on pinot grigio that had been kept in the freezer until it reached "slush" consistency, you could say I was something of a train wreck.

It was the annual Denver Derby, a flimsy excuse for a party that attracts drunks of all types: wives who hate their husbands, husbands who hate their wives, twentysomethings looking to drink dark liquor and fight (Hello! Jackson Tilley, nice to meet you!), horse lovers, horse haters (you should see what they do to the losers), and every manner of person in between. The Denver Derby isn't about fancy hats or even about watching the *actual* Kentucky Derby, taking place some 1,200 miles away. It's about getting blackout drunk, arguing with the people you love in liquor store parking lots, and whispering *"bad friend!"* over and over again as your roommate tries to entertain company in a shared living space. Oh, wait…I'm sorry. That's just what the derby meant *to me*. I'd spent the better part of the morning drinking mint juleps and popping Xanax, the traditional spring ritual of fellow housewives across the country. Suddenly, faster than you could say American Pharoah, it was two in the morning and I'd managed to start a fight with every one of my friends. These weren't normal fights.This was fighting of the "I hate you and never want to see you again" variety, the inevitable conclusion of introducing bourbon into my bloodstream.

I wish I could offer more details about May 3. I wish, for my own sake, that I had a more concrete grasp on the events of the fourth, or the fifth, or even the sixth. May 3 started as many other days had over the previous six months. Still partially dressed, I peeled myself away from my sheets, face stuck to a pillow. I'd reach to the bedside table, instinctively knowing where my pill case slept at night, feel around and withdraw a few of the little green footballs one by one. They say that amputees can still feel a tingle where their limbs used to be— that's how I felt about Xanax. Even if it hadn't yet found its way into my system, if I really thought about it, I could almost conjure up the sensation of their effect. After a few unsuccessful attempts, I pulled myself out of bed and went through my normal ritual after a hellacious night of drinking: brush teeth, cry; shower, cry; piss, cry; take another Xanax, cry; put on robe and swear to never do this again, cry. Then do it again. This is the life of an addict, or at the very least, the life of this addict.

It wasn't until I walked out of my bedroom and saw the look of disgust on my roommate's face that the gravity of my situation set in. Though I couldn't remember it, what had transpired the day before had been worse than any of my other drunken antics. She told me she was heading out to run errands, and I sat on the couch to try and resurrect a few memories. What scraps I could recall, I didn't like. Ask any addict what emotion they felt most often while in the throes of their addiction, and they will say shame. Shame, to me, is more than an emotion. It's an old friend, perhaps my oldest. Shame kept me company at night when I was alone, and shame woke up next to me each morning. On this bright and sunny day in May, the shame had reached its boiling point. I'd vowed to stop abusing pills and I'd promised myself I would try to drink like a normal adult. Neither happened, of course, and in what seemed like a nanosecond, I'd found myself, once again, completely out of control.

Shame brewed in my body like coffee in a French press. It started as a few grounds in the bottom, bitter and dark, and then came the boiling water, heating up the whole mixture to near-critical levels, until *wham*, like a bolt of lightning, some force pressed down hard and mixed it all together, into some dark, potent brew ready to scald the first person who came in contact with it. My shame and anxiety had boiled over, and I thought it was probably better to just end it all. I'd failed at trying to wean myself off drugs more times than I could count, and I couldn't bear the idea of having to come clean about the full extent of my addiction. Rather dramatically, I called the elevator and made my way up to our rooftop, where I'd decided I'd leap off, drink in hand, like the opening scene from *The First Wives Club*. I stood up on the ledge and looked down. For the first time in my life, I felt in control of my own destiny, and it frightened me. I took another step forward and thought, *better get a good look*. Suddenly, music started playing from one of the apartments below me. "Tainted Love," by Soft Cell. That song had been my mother's ringtone for about three years of my childhood, so anytime it plays,

I am instantly reminded of her (and yes, I fully acknowledge that it's an odd choice for ringtone, but the heart wants what the heart wants). The music kept playing, and at the risk of sounding even more insane, it felt for a moment like the clouds opened up above me. I'd later learn in AA that this is known as the moment of clarity—a fleeting moment that happens concurrently with hitting rock bottom, where you suddenly know what you need to do. I stepped down from the ledge, took the elevator back to my apartment, and made two phone calls.

The first call is a blur, likely as a result of the five additional Xanax I'd swallowed the moment I walked in my door. I telephoned my parents and through tears told them that I was suicidal (not a drug addict, though, one step at a time, please) and that I needed to go to rehab. Being the kind, loving parents that they are, they didn't question why someone with a mental health issue would need to go to rehab, or why my words were slurred so early in the morning. They told me they loved me and would be at my apartment in three hours to take me home with them while we figured out what to do. The next call was to Jeremy, the cofounder of the company. I told him I was going to need some time off to go to rehab for my "depression" in order to get to the bottom of what was causing me to feel this way (spoiler alert: it was the drugs).

"Jeremy, I think I need help. I want to die, and I don't know what to do about it." The words stung as they left my mouth. "You have to do what you have to do. Go get help, and we'll be here waiting for you," he replied warmly. These were some of the most intense moments of love I'd ever felt. Never had I expected to have been met with such open acceptance and support for something I had felt so deeply ashamed of for so many years. It was like coming out all over again, only this time, as someone with a disease. I hung up the phone and started to pack my bags. Into a few monogrammed suitcases, I stuffed some framed photos and all the athleisure wear I could find. (I'd recently watched the Lindsay Lohan docuseries on

OWN about life after rehab, so I had already subconsciously planned my outfits in the months leading up.) I swallowed a few more Xanax (for those keeping count, we're up to fifteen for the day, about half of my record) and grabbed my laptop.

"BEST OCEANFRONT CELEBRITY REHAB CENTER." I still have the screenshots from the second week of treatment, when I opened my computer to find that phrase entered into the search window on my browser. I certainly wasn't a celebrity, but clearly *Lindsay* on OWN had inspired me. Two options had popped up— Passages Malibu, a facility that didn't require its clients to attend AA meetings and claimed to have found the "cure" for addiction and Promises Malibu, perhaps the most famous of all treatment centers for its celebrity clientele and pioneering "Malibu method," which combines a holistic approach to treatment with traditional twelve-step programs. AA wasn't for me, as I'd decided that I hated God and couldn't spend the rest of my life drinking bad coffee and sitting in church basements. I sent the link for Passages to my mom, and she went to work booking me a bed.

After a tearful goodbye with my father in Denver, my mom and I made our way to Malibu. She dropped me off and helped me get settled. It was clear to us, however, that she shouldn't linger so she started to prepare herself for the separation. My mother's anxiety about leaving me was palpable. A bomb had just been dropped on her, and though it still wasn't clear to me, she knew I was an addict. I think she thought that if she stayed any longer, I might tell her I was leaving too. We both knew that couldn't happen. Another client, a woman about the same age as my mother, hugged her and told her that I would be okay. She said she had kids of her own, and that while leaving was hard, it was the right thing to do. With a kiss on the forehead and an "I'm proud of you," my mom got into the back of a black Yukon XL and headed to the airport.

In the twenty-four hours leading up to check-in, I'd taken roughly thirty Xanax, drank at least one shot of every type of liquor

I could get at the airport bar, and smoked enough weed to ensure I'd still reek of it by the time I arrived. I have only faint memories of both traveling from Colorado to California and the initial process at Passages. The first several days were a mix of anxiety and sadness about what I'd done. The cat was out of the bag and it was clawing the drapes. I was put on a mix of Librium, Ativan, and clonidine—a drug cocktail used to prevent seizures resulting from withdrawal. I couldn't stand up straight and I talked to a lawn statue of a tortoise for several days in a row, thinking it was real. Finally, I woke up on the fifth day with a throbbing headache and a hole in my lip, the result of accidentally stabbing myself in the face with a fork, while trying to eat as I was suffering from delirium tremens. The house manager was knocking on my bedroom door. "Get dressed. It's meeting time!"

Fuck, I thought. I'd picked this place because they *didn't* believe in AA. They had the cure to addiction, and I assumed I could largely go about my life without structure or supervision. Surprise, surprise! Someone blacked out on pills isn't well equipped to differentiate between two similarly named treatment facilities. Lo and behold, I'd sent the phone number of *Promises* Malibu, not *Passages* Malibu, to my mother and ended up in a treatment center wildly different from the one I'd planned on attending. They say that the universe works in mysterious ways, and Promises turned out to be the perfect place for me. It was everything I'd wanted in a treatment center—bougie amenities like horseback riding and tennis lessons, a chef, swimming pools, and a mix of interesting clientele. If I was going to get sober, I at least wanted to be comfortable.

Sitting in a treatment room, the sound of white noise was deafening. My therapist was going over my post-treatment plan with me, and she had some concerns. I hadn't yet admitted I was an alcoholic and a drug addict, and we were nearly two weeks into treatment. More concerning was the fact that I had agreed to no longer drink but refused to budge on the notion of giving up smoking weed. This is where I think most people's questions often arise about my own struggle with addiction. How can a person advocate for the consumption of marijuana without consuming it? It was a question I struggled with for months. With so much of my identity tied up in my career, how could I rectify these two conflicting ideologies? Would I be able to quit consuming cannabis and emerge from the front gates of my beloved Malibu rehab center a gay, sober, (legal) weed dealer? It dawned on me that if I really wanted to get better, I'd need to fully commit myself to being sober. I decided that I'd try it for three months, and if I hated it, I could always go back to using. Halfway through treatment, I vowed to no longer use substances of any kind and finally, at a seven o'clock meeting one morning, said the magic words in a room full of strangers: "I'm Jackson, and I'm an addict."

Forty-five days passed and I checked out of treatment, boarded a flight, and flew home to Denver. My first day back at work was a nightmare. I stood in the alley and sobbed into my boss's shoulders, ruining a beautiful silk blouse she'd worn for my homecoming. I spent the first three hours at the office contemplating what a relapse might look like and "played the tape forward," as they say. It wouldn't have ended well. One of my best friends, Barbie, telephoned and told me she'd just moved into a new house off Mulholland Drive and I could live with her if I thought it might help. I didn't know it at the time, but she saved my life and gave me an existence worth living. It occurred to me that I wasn't meant to be living in Colorado while newly sober. My sober friends, my AA meetings, and my support system were all in Los Angeles. I couldn't believe, after the hell that was living in LA the first time, I was even contemplating moving back.

I brought the idea up to my bosses, and they told me to take as much time as I needed. I have to think that had I worked in any other organization, I would've likely lost my job and been told to pack my things. I couldn't believe I was asking for another leave of absence. Panic filled my body as the words left my mouth—a month of introspection had left me unable to read others because I was so hyper-focused on myself. This group had gone to incredible lengths not just to get me sober, but to keep me sober. Their kindness wasn't lost on me, and I felt like saying I needed more time would disappoint them. But it wasn't the case. The cannabis industry and our company in particular consists of a group of people destined to change the world, to bring relief to those who need it, and to empower people to exercise their own personal freedoms. Such was the case with my sobriety. I had the full support of our entire organization as I walked out the front doors of the office bound once again for sunny Los Angeles. They hugged me goodbye, and for the second time in two months, told me to take the time I needed.

A friend of a friend had offered the use of a friend of a friend of her father's private plane, apparently sympathetic to my fear of drinking on a commercial airplane after barely a month of sobriety. I headed to the Centennial Airport, snapped a picture in front of it, and posted it to Instagram with the caption "They tried to make me go to rehab, and I said 'chic, when's my flight?'" Thus, my triumphant return to Los Angeles, a new, sober man, was announced to friends and strangers alike. Just like Miley sang it, I hopped off the plane at LAX, and made my way to my new home. Though I wasn't able to keep my old job, my bosses had arranged for a new one that I could do remotely, the most glamorous position of all, running the weekend customer chat line for people having technical issues with their vape pens. Sick. I went from social media manager to customer service associate in two months flat—the first unintentional demotion of my short career. Somehow, it didn't matter. It gave me the chance to attend meetings during the day, earn a modest wage, and focus on healing myself after years of mental and physical damage.

I'm a perennial busybody, so the idea of getting glimpses into the lives of the people who use our products through short, sometimes unintelligible responses on our live chat affected me in a way I hadn't expected. It was an opportunity to gauge the habits of people from all around the world. I often wondered if anyone could imagine that the person they were chatting with was fresh from an AA meeting, having just shared their struggles with staying clean. As customers struggled to use their vape pens, I struggled to avoid using them. They made asking for help seem so easy, when for me, muttering "I need help" through cracking vocal cords was the most difficult thing I'd ever done. Waking up in cold sweats after nightmares of a relapse, I'd yearn for a solution as simple as the one I offered our customers. "Turn it off, and turn it back on again. That should do the trick." If only sobriety were so simple. The conversations were short and no one knew me. It was like an online AA meeting, except we were chatting about damaged products instead of damaged people. Then during the day, instead of faulty devices, I spent my time discussing faulty synapses that had yet to be repaired. If I could have popped my brain into a prepaid mailer and returned it to the factory maybe I wouldn't have needed to attend meetings anymore. Sadly, the brain and the body don't come with a lifetime warranty, so off to a church basement I went. I was living parallel, anonymous lives. One online with consumers of cannabis, and one in real life with those searching for a way to stay sober. I was humbled in a way I hadn't been before, taken back to the core of what I had set out to do in the first place. I was sober, and for the first time in a long time, I was relating to other people. Nothing else really mattered.

Eventually, it hit me that I couldn't continue working in the cannabis industry. I was struggling to rectify the moral quandary of how to peddle ancillary cannabis hardware on the weekends, while speaking at meetings and working with a sponsor during the week. I told my bosses that I was going to look for another job and, with their blessing, went out hunting. Within a week, I'd been offered a job working on social media and PR for a gay dating app, one which you've probably heard of. I walked in the door on my first day, bright-eyed and bushy-tailed, only to be smacked in the face with seven inches of reality—I missed my old job. I didn't make it fifteen minutes before I began plotting how I could make a return. My old human resources department hadn't even filed my resignation letter yet, and still I knew this new place wasn't right for me. The dating app office was total chaos, a living hell for someone who was still suffering from post-acute withdrawal syndrome, the main side effect of which was an inability to stand for more than ten minutes without toppling over like a pile of Jenga blocks. They had assigned me the task of researching celebrity influencers for whom we might gift a premium version of the app as a marketing ploy. Then it hit me—why wasn't this being done in the cannabis space? We'd dabbled in it a bit a few months prior, so why not develop an entire department around celebrity gifting? I telephoned my boss and pitched him on the idea. "What about coming back to work at a cannabis company?" he asked me. "We'd love to have you back, but I worry that it could jeopardize your sobriety." In the second moment of clarity in just two short months, I suddenly knew the answer to my problems.

It became crystal clear that cannabis wasn't the issue, nor was it drugs or alcohol. I guess sixty days of meetings must've begun to work, because it finally set in that *I was the problem*. It was *my own* addiction issue that meant I couldn't drink or use again. We live in a world where alcohol flows freely, weed is easier to buy than it is to consume, and recreational drugs can be found in any bar or club around the country. If I wanted to get back to living a normal life, it suddenly made sense that it wasn't my surroundings that needed to change, it was me. And change I did.

Three days into my new job, I started carrying my possessions out to my car, one at a time so as not to arouse any undue suspicion about the scheme now percolating in my mind. At five on a Friday afternoon, I put my company computer and keycard in the drawer of my desk, walked out the front door, and hit send on an email. My letter of resignation went out with a *whoosh*, and so ended my seventy-two-hour stint working in the gay dating world. I set up a desk outside my bedroom at Barbie's house and, with the blessings of my bosses and an offer letter with wet ink, set out to develop the first celebrity gifting program in the cannabis world. With AA books in hand, so began a new life as the thing I'd thought impossible: a sober weed dealer.

First, it was time to lease a new sports car (hey, it was LA after all).

CHAPTER 7

[REDACTED]

It had been about a month since my departure from the wild world of weed, and baby, I was back. In what seemed like an instant, I dove headfirst into sobriety while launching an entirely new career within the company. Officially, my new title was VIP Relations, and I was tasked with getting our products into the hands of tastemakers. Based in Los Angeles, I was well positioned to launch this new program, but there was one issue: I didn't know a damn soul working in the entertainment industry. Not to worry, I told myself. Again, and forgive me for repeating this, but when it comes to knowing other people's business, I reign supreme. My title should really have been Chief Yenta, but VIP Relations would have to work in the interim. With an Excel sheet open on my computer screen, I set about making a list of every celebrity who had publicly spoken about using cannabis. From there, I created new tabs—a "maybe" category, for people who I just assumed were stoners but had never actually said it, and a list of "reaches," consisting of people like, you know, Barack Obama. No cannabis company had ever created an entire department around the idea of celebrity gifting, though I had many friends who worked in fashion, where the practice is essential to business models. It's fairly simple: gift a product to a celebrity, pray that they enjoy it enough to use it in their daily lives, and wait for them to talk about it or be photographed with it.

The issues with my plan quickly became apparent. I purchased a subscription to ContactAnyCelebrity.com, a website whose URL alone fails to inspire confidence, and each time I copied a name from my Excel sheet into the search bar, I was met with the same result. Listing after listing named only one point of contact: an agent. If I was going to create a buzz with celebrities, it became clear that I'd need to start from the inside and work my way out. Using the latest issue of *Variety*, I quickly began noting the names of agents who seemed to be doing more deals than others. From there, I pieced together something of an organization chart, in order to see which agents made up each group within the agency. It wasn't going to be just a matter of sending gifts blindly. I needed to make it clear that we had something everyone wanted, and the only way to get it, *was through me*. I placed an order for a thousand custom-engraved O.penVAPE batteries from our warehouse. Within a week, the pens arrived, emblazoned with a custom monogram for each agent and an imprint of their corporate logo. In the living room of her Beverly Glen home, I recruited Barbie to help me assemble the gift boxes. I should mention at this point that, with Barbie, I'd found my soulmate. She's a sixtysomething, Nice Jewish Lady™ from Orange County, who shares my love of shopping, reality TV, and dining out rather than eating in. We tuned the TV to *The Wendy Williams Show,* and went to work filling box after box with bright green containers with the engraved pens. They were tied tight with a bow and stacked fifty-high in the living room. It looked like the gift wrap area at Bloomingdale's on Christmas Eve. Now, each box needed to come with a personalized note and a business card. My handwriting looks like that of a three-year-old, so though the cards came from me, they were lovingly written in Barbie's practiced cursive. As you're reading this, I'm sure you must be thinking, *How sweet. He sent gift boxes*

to everyone at each of the companies he was trying to gain access to.
You couldn't be more wrong. Instead, I handpicked about 70 percent
of the people who made up each department and sent gift boxes to
only "the chosen few." I was determined to make these products *the*
gift that everyone *had* to have.

We loaded up my new car (Black C-Class AMG—I was an Ange-
leno now, thank you very much) and hit the agencies. We drove
from Santa Monica to Beverly Hills to Century City and everywhere
in between. Mailroom after mailroom, I began planting the seeds of
our company. By five o'clock on Friday afternoon, I'd delivered some
300 boxes across the city.

Monday morning came around and my inbox was flooded.
There were countless emails thanking me for the gift, and for every
thank you, there were half a dozen requests asking to be included
in the next round. Person after person reached out to inquire as
to how they could obtain a gift box for their clients. My plan was
working. I telephoned my bosses to let them know the good news.
It was pure Hollywood magic. I still remember one of my bosses
saying, "Only you." In a seventy-two-hour period, I'd gone from not
knowing a single person in the industry to having an inside line with
the movers and shakers of the most impactful cultural machine in
America, the entertainment industry. We had something everyone
wanted and that something was weed.

So began a chain reaction of supply and demand. For every box
that went out, ten requests came in. What follows is a true account
of just a couple events that happened in the following weeks and
months, presented in the style of Special Counsel Robert S. Mueller
III, with names and identifying info redacted to protect the Hollywood elites still in the cannabis closet.

One afternoon, I received a phone call from ███████, who
was working for one of LA's biggest agencies, ███████. One of
their biggest clients, Academy Award–winner ███████ had
expressed an interest in receiving a gift box. I picked up the phone

and instantly recognized both the person on the other line and the client they represented. Though it was a gift box they wanted, I was warned: "We will happily accept on behalf of ███████████, but please know that if it comes out in the press that we did so, ███████████ will vehemently deny it." I hung up the phone, and it began to sink in what we'd accomplished. We had managed to create artificial demand for a product and boy, was demand skyrocketing.

Shortly thereafter, we were contacted by one of social media's most familiar faces, ███████████, who was interested in exploring a custom cannabis line and asked if some representatives of our company would mind flying in for a meeting. In short order, I was boarding a plane and preparing a pitch for the next great celebrity cannabis line. We arrived to pandemonium, as word had spread that the fabled weed-man cometh. Glancing around the office, I noticed that everyone already knew my name, where I worked, and what I did. Who'd have fucking thought? Question after question was hurled my way, as the group frantically tried to figure out a way to acquire gift boxes of their own. The meeting with ███████████ wrapped, and I went back toward Los Angeles, inbox bursting with more and more requests as I left.

Some weeks later, I was invited to a taping of Golden Globe–winner and ███████████-about-town ███████████'s new television show. While waiting backstage, ███████████ ran up to me, threw ███████████ arms around me, and thanked me preemptively for the gift. A few feet away, I recognized ███████████, the president of the very network on whose soundstage we were standing. "I'd recognize those green boxes anywhere!" Yes, even the president of the network had heard of our gifting program, and he was adamant about being placed on the list for the next gifting event.

In a matter of months, I'd managed to snoop around online and gather enough information to build a sizable book of contacts consisting of the most recognized names in Hollywood. Though we may not be able to run ads or write off our expenses, we could certainly build a name for ourselves in the highest rungs of culture. What does any of this mean in the larger context of society? It's not just a chance to humble brag about my networking abilities (though, shout-out to me) but rather a testament to the changing tides in the social fabric of California.

In late 2015, billboards began popping up all along California's highways advertising new and different marijuana companies and their various products. The recent passage of several assembly bills allowing for advertising of any kind altered the landscape for medical marijuana across the state, a sign of increased acceptance. In October 2015, the law firm Harris Bricken published an overview of the assembly bills, also known as the California Medical Marijuana Regulation and Safety Act, or MMRSA. In short, the report found that the passage of these bills created several fundamental changes to the infrastructure in which medical marijuana businesses operated:

1. MMRSA legalized all commercial cannabis operations pursuant to local laws and subject to permitting restrictions;

2. Prior to now, only nonprofit "collectives," as discussed in previous chapters, were authorized to sell cannabis. Now, for-profit entities were also allowed to jump into the game;

3. It established the Bureau of Medical Marijuana Regulations, an agency with the authority to enforce new restrictions and monitor the overall health of the industry;

4. The bills called for the California Department of Public Health to establish guidelines for testing and labeling of marijuana products;

5. And, most importantly (with the exception of the City of Los Angeles), empowered local municipalities to create and enforce their own regulations surrounding the dispensing of medical cannabis in compliance with state law.

MMRSA was obviously much more complex, but for our purposes, a cursory discussion will suffice. It also begins to explain why, in the fall of 2015, cannabis seemingly defied logic and became *even more popular* in California. More and more dispensaries opened in cannabis-friendly cities, and relaxed advertising regulations allowed for billboards across the state to host cannabis content. Thanks in large part to the loosening of regulations, some years later our own company even ran its own set of ads leading up to awards season in tandem with a *Variety* article about Organa Brands. The ad copy: "Meet your new red carpet companion."

Our company wasn't alone in finding new success in a state long criticized for its unreasonably complex legal and regulatory framework. By mid-2015, the national cannabis market, wholesale and retail combined, was expected to reach $3.2 billion, according to the *Marijuana Business Factbook,* with California making up 49 percent of all cannabis sales. It was becoming increasingly clear to those both in and adjacent to the industry that cannabis businesses weren't going anywhere. And while California would prove to still be two years away from passing recreational marijuana reform, the new medical rules created the framework for businesses to start operating outside of the shadows.

Look no further than the landscape of California dispensaries. Suddenly, the clientele was markedly upscale, demanding more of a luxury shopping experience—far removed from the surfers crowding dimly lit Venice Beach storefronts. I was blown away upon entering a bright, shining example of a new wave cannabis dispensary on Sunset Boulevard. It was more akin to an Apple Store than a head shop. It was the first time I can recall seeing real, physical evidence that the industry was changing, and surprisingly, it was for the better. If cannabis was no longer a taboo subject, that meant the business was evolving. After all, there are only two options when it comes to survival: adapt or die.

Though cannabis had begun to see the light across the state, it wasn't the case in all circles. I'd settled into a nice routine attending AA meetings in the evenings, spending time with other alcoholics and addicts. I largely attended meetings in Malibu and West Hollywood, almost always a stone's throw away from the dispensaries I frequented as part of my networking efforts. The first time I shared that I was both sober and working in the marijuana industry, I could feel an icy mist fall over the room. It was more than my fellow AAs just having moral quandaries about someone in their ranks encouraging cannabis use. I later came to find out that the real issue was rooted in a tinge of jealousy because few dared to enter a dispensary for fear of what might happen. Meanwhile, I had a home office stuffed to the brim with marijuana products, and the thought of using them never crossed my mind. It also made just as much sense why the owners of the company had trusted me with such a huge supply of products since the cardinal rule of the drug world is "don't get high on your own supply." They'd found someone who not only had no interest in using the products, but had a built-in support system to avoid it.

The cannabis industry is extraordinarily complex. So complex, in fact, that almost all traditional means of sales, advertising, and bill pay were, at the time, unavailable. While it may seem insane to dedicate one's workday entirely to giving custom vape pens to celebrities, innovation is born out of necessity. The most thrilling part of working in an industry like this is that, more often than not, when executing a plan of action, it's the first time such a scheme has been contemplated. It's a brand new industry built on firsts. From cannabis ads plastered on billboards along the freeway to cannabis events being held at Coachella or pop-up dispensaries opening in hotel chains, in our industry, these things have simply never been done before.

It's also important to note just how key these changes have been with regard to the stigma around cannabis use. Though California was the first state to legalize medical marijuana, it didn't happen without its fair share of struggles. In a 2015 study from the *Journal of Psychoactive Drugs* by Dr. Travis Satterlund, researchers conducted a survey of several medical marijuana patients in California. When the respondents were surveyed in 2009, so intense was the stigma that most wouldn't even seek a cannabis prescription from their general physician. One responded "there was obviously that kind of negative stigma of using marijuana that I'd be looked upon as kind of an addict or a drug user more than a patient." Another said: "I worked for many years for my employer, and I was more concerned about them finding out about this; that's why I didn't start treatment sooner. I was concerned about the stigma. My job requires total concentration and focus and I wouldn't want people to think that my marijuana use would interfere with that, or my ability to do that." It's hard to believe the changes that occurred in such a short window from 2009 to 2016, but this was happening all across the country. Shame and fear had been replaced by acceptance, and there was no better example than California. Whereas just a few years prior, people had feared for their jobs as a result of their cannabis use, by this point, tens of thousands of Americans across the country were gainfully employed as a result of marijuana. I spoke to Daryn Carp, media expert and chief of staff for Andy Cohen, who I think summed up the shift nicely, telling me:

> Most people are either open about smoking pot, or know someone close to them who does. You can be athletic, smart, and successful and smoke weed daily. Most people were scared of the unknown and cannabis was mostly unknown—we didn't know the dangers. Now, decades later, it's being used medically, and people aren't as scared to use it. It is much less dangerous than alcohol and cigarettes, and those are completely normalized in our culture. Weed is the next big thing.

And as for the gifting program? In the first year, I completed more than a thousand gifting events, placing our products into the hands of celebrities across the state. By the end of the year, one of our most successful events centered around creating custom gift boxes to be given as wedding party gifts at ███████ 's wedding. Inside each box was a pen engraved with their hashtag to mark the event—and, of course, one of my business cards. After all, what's the point in giving a gift if the recipient doesn't know who gave it? The cannabis industry was maturing at a rapid pace, and we held the evidence of it in our hands in the form of thank-you notes from celebrities and customers alike.

INTERVIEW WITH CHRIS MCELVANY

Chris McElvany is one of the cofounders of Organa Brands. Obsessed with science and horticulture, he popularized modern cannabis extraction methods and created a framework for the responsible research and development of cutting-edge cannabis products. He runs Organa Labs, the longest-licensed cannabis extraction facility in the country. Even as someone who works in this industry, I'm often confused by the nuances of cannabis extracts and how they get to the shelves. Chris is one of the foremost authorities on the subject, and I spoke with him to help clarify some of the mystery.

In layman's terms, can you walk me through the extraction process?

The extraction process is actually very simple. In fact, it's not much different than brewing tea. With tea brewing, the desired finished product includes the solvent, water, and the extract of tea combined together. With cannabis extracts, we remove the solvent as a final step. In most of the facilities we operate around the world, we use carbon dioxide as a solvent instead of water, since CO_2 can be "tuned" to extract most of the product we want and leave behind the parts of the plant that we don't. A familiar example in fact, are chlorophyll(s). As you may know, this is why plants appear green. Since these molecules are soluble in water and less soluble in CO_2, they can be easily removed in our preliminary extraction process. We use liquid CO_2 (subcritical), or supercritical CO_2 since gasses are very weak solvents. CO_2 is also very easy to separate from our extract, since it is a gas at normal atmospheric conditions and quickly boils off during the process when operating pressures are returned to normal. In the simplest of terms, that's all we are doing. Of course, we further process the extract to achieve the desired final product to ensure higher safety and enjoyment for various means of consumption.

How have things changed, from a scientific perspective, in the last ten years?

There have been major developments and improvements around the equipment used for extraction, as well as the cultivars that grow it. Cannabis breeding, until recently, has been done for the most part "illegally" and somewhat isolated from many of the modern advancements in normal agriculture practices and technology, though this has not stopped or likely even slowed the development of new strains or cultivars. In fact, the opposite is probably more true. The illegality of cannabis breeding, has fortunately led to more widespread and numerous individual breeding projects and the diversification of the cannabis phenotypes, meaning more varieties. The opposite is true of most agricultural products we consume and is evidenced by the number of choices we find for produce in our grocery stores. Maybe few of us would appreciate hundreds of different flavors of broccoli anyway. Though for cannabis, we are fortunate.

What's the most misunderstood notion when it comes to the science of cannabis or cannabis extraction?

That the plant or the science is new. This is a plant that has been around since before recorded history and likely as long, if not longer, than humans have existed. We have evolved alongside the plant and with the plant. There is a great book written by one of my favorite authors, Michael Pollan, called *The Botany of Desire*. Pollan does a great job of articulating the relationship humans and cannabis have had throughout history, and how we have evolved together. It begs further conversation and urgency around the plant being illegal. Cannabis isn't new and has been part of our life and our diets until recently, when it was prohibited by modern governments. As an example, imagine the outrage and health decline in society as a whole if our governments took aim at the citrus industry next and prohibited vitamin C.

How did you find yourself working in cannabis for a living?

I found myself compelled to join the industry when I realized how unjust cannabis prohibition was, and how important the plant was to our health.

Why has potency become such a hot topic in recent years?

Potency will always be important to some consumers as it's a measure of the utility in intoxication to some extent. The more potent, the more intoxicating effects one can achieve. Of course, intoxication or effect is subjective, and only one of the many qualities the plant possesses. More discerning consumers typically find a balance between flavor and potency, and enjoy the nuanced effect of the cannabinoids, terpenes, and flavonoids. The plant is truly a flavor and drug factory, ripe for exploration. Those who seek only the most potent varieties of cannabis are missing out.

Do you see federal legalization happening in the near future?

I thought it would have happened years ago. It must be coming soon, I would think. We will see some major progress going into the next presidential elections. Only a foolish politician would run against the movement at this point. People have figured out that it's not the evil plant that the last few generations have led us to believe it was. It would be inhumane and unethical to continue down the path of criminalization knowing that our health as a human race depends on it.

What needs to happen to get to that point?

The old guard in Congress needs to pass or be replaced. We have a select few regulators that are holding onto their biased and fraudulent beliefs or positions. I won't name names for fear of being targeted.

Walk me through the basics of cannabis—what about the plant creates the effect in our systems?

We have a natural endocannabinoid system that the plant has evolved and been evolved to interact with. It is intertwined with pretty much every other biological system in the human, and in fact, animal kingdom's, body. Again, it's part of our evolutionary makeup. The plant produces a host of cannabinoids that act on our biological systems in different ways. What was first? The endocannabinoid system and our natural endogenous endocannabinoid anandamide or the plant? I think, and Pollan would have you believe, that it all evolved together.

What does the future look like? What processes and breakthroughs do you think we can expect to see in the next ten years?

I think you will see greater efficiencies and scalability with cultivation and processing. We will see increased entry from drug developers and pharmaceutical companies and likely greater access to synthetic, or non-natural cannabis products and formulations. We will likely see a branch in the industry so to speak, where continually diversified "craft"-like cannabis plants and products exist alongside more commercialized products. The breakthroughs will likely be spread over both sides. Current selective breeding progress will continue and uncover many amazing varieties of plants, and drug developers will work to create amazing new drug products in tandem. In summary, there will be breakthroughs all around us, as the science has been stalled for a few decades. There is much room to catch up to drug development and modern agricultural processes.

CHAPTER 8

Price Per Barrel

The most expensive oil on Earth costs $144 million dollars per barrel. You might assume that we're talking about truffle oil or petroleum, but you would be wrong. It's cannabis oil, made by extracting compounds from the cannabis plant using a variety of chemical processes. This isn't new. Indeed, cannabis and its extracts have existed in general pharmacopeia for thousands of years. Prior to 1937, before cannabis became federally illegal, it was commonplace to walk into a pharmacy and purchase a vial of "marihuana tincture" from behind the counter. It was often prescribed for a malady known as *female hysteria*—the Founding Fathers apparently thought weed a better solution than, say, giving women the right to vote or own property. Later, documents from the infamous MK-Ultra project of the 1960s revealed that the CIA had used cigarettes laced with cannabis oil to extract information from unwitting suspects. I don't know much about interrogation, but I have to imagine it's hard to get useful intel from someone who just wants to eat Baked Alaska and watch *Bewitched*. Perhaps the earliest iteration of modern cannabis extracts, often called hash oil, was popularized in D. Gold's 1973 book *Cannabis Alchemy: The Art of Modern Hashmaking*. It was a clumsy process that involved running cannabis flowers through alcohol and a charcoal filter to reveal a honey-like substance that could be smoked or ingested.

Modern applications of cannabis extracts are vastly different than their historical counterparts. Imagine you've just decided to embark on the *Whole30* diet. In front of you sits a giant bowl of Nutella, in this case a metaphor for the cannabis flower as a whole. Chocolate, oil, sugar, and hazelnuts, the components that make up the substance, dare not touch your lips or you'll be banned from your Instagram community of fellow crash dieters. Instead of devouring the bowl in one breathless gulp, imagine using a combination of liquids and gasses to force each ingredient apart from one another, until you're left with just the hazelnuts, the highest value portion of Nutella, and also an approved part of any millennial diet. This is supercritical fluid extraction, or SFE, the most common extraction method used in the cannabis industry. The process was all the rage in other applications in the early 1970s and was thought to be the next big thing in removing fat from foods. It's the same process used when taking a lavender flower and refining it into the end-product that ultimately finds its way into a seventy-five-dollar diptyque candle. The application of this process to cannabis contributed to a boom in the industry and is at the core of the business model of many of the largest cannabis producers in America.

Anyone who's ever walked through a dispensary tends to describe it in much the same way: overwhelming. Regardless of whether you're shopping in the Apple Store–like mecca that is Medmen or a smaller mom-and-pop off the beaten path, one thing is certain—consumers have an almost unlimited number of choices, ranging from infused tampons to traditional edibles and vape pens. The dispensary landscape has shifted immensely over the last five years, as more and more consumers gravitate toward less traditional means of consumption, like edibles, topicals, and vaporizers. Hell, you can even buy a THC inhaler if that suits your needs. Cannabis currently exists in a gray area. Despite being legal in more states than not, the lack of federal regulation has created small pockets of producers existing within an opaque patchwork of cannabis laws. The result is a mixture of quality, brands, and potency, all sold side-by-side, on the same shelves, in the same storefronts. What you might find in a dispensary in Los Angeles will be wildly different than what you might find just a few miles away in Orange County. The same is true in many of the other thirty-two states with some form of legalized cannabis. At face value, it seems that there are almost no unifying characteristics running through any of these markets. Dispensaries are filled with a vast assortment of cannabis products, many sold with no rhyme or reason. When you look deeper, though, it becomes clear just exactly how this product mix came to be—its cannabis oil.

From the start, cannabis oil was an alternative to the traditional consumption method, smoking. Cannabis flowers were grown, trimmed, and dried. They'd then be sold to consumers, who would grind up the crystallized nuggets and roll them into a joint or put them into a bong. While still popular, the market has seen a shift away from this method of consumption, instead opting for methods that are trendier, or perceived to be cleaner, all of which are powered by cannabis oil extract. In Colorado in 2014, dried cannabis flower accounted for 61 percent of sales. By 2018, that number was down to 44 percent, according to a recent study from BDS Analytics. In that same period, the sale of concentrates more than doubled, to 31 percent. Take for example, the O.penVAPE device that since 2014, according to BDS Analytics, has been the number two best-selling cannabis brand in the history of legal sales. When the device was first introduced in 2012, it was nothing short of a miracle. It took the best aspect of the traditional method (getting high) and launched it into the twenty-first century with clever packaging, tech-forward hardware, and an experience that was nearly odorless. For the modern cannabis consumer, it was a game changer. As the years went on, the science behind cannabis extraction became increasingly complex, and the resulting products safer and more efficient. It became clear that this glistening cannabis extract could be used in any number of applications, and the resulting product development resulted in a marked uptick in the range of products available. Gone were the days of sparking up a loose joint, replaced instead by a sleek vape pen for daytime use, an artisan chocolate truffle before bed, and—if the late night edible didn't put you to sleep—cannabis-infused lubes and sprays that have grown popular among those seeking new and interesting ways to add spice to their sex lives. Recent data suggests why the shift away from smoking may be occurring. According to the Colorado Department of Public Health and Environment, "Some research shows that vaporizers lower the amount of potentially harmful tars in smoke. Other studies have shown fewer respiratory symptoms among those using vaporizers." That said, many of these studies should be taken with a grain of salt, as there is not enough long-term research to say definitively that vaporizing is the safest means of consumption. This is yet another argument in favor federal legalization, as we likely won't see long-term, government-backed studies on either the efficacy or safety of long-term cannabis use until such legislation occurs.

On awakening, there are CBD bath bombs and shower scrubs, infused facial creams that claim to halt the aging process, medicated lip balms that can rid the body of cold sores, and even marijuana-infused candles for those who don't think their living room smells quite dank enough. The list of products goes on, and with good reason. They sell. A dispensary is not unlike a grocery store, in that shelf space is valuable and only those products that convert to sales are able to maintain a footprint. About five years ago, a website called Rules of the Internet popped up and laid out some ground rules for life in our digital age. Some were satirical, others genuine. In discussing the selections of cannabis products that fill the market, I'm reminded of *Rule 34: There is a porn version of it, no exceptions.*

I'd like to propose an addition to that rule for the cannabis age: *Rule 34.1: There is a weed version of it, no exceptions.*

I was recently in a dispensary in Denver giving a tour to some advertising executives who were working on a new project. For many, it was their first time stepping foot into a dispensary. A quick count showed more than 300 products in a store that was barely 1,000 square feet. The bulk of the products carry various brand names, but the reality is, that almost all of them originate from just a handful of producers. Does this sound familiar? If you've ever stepped into a liquor store, it should. Much like our intoxicant counterparts in the regulated liquor industry, the illusion of choice powers a great deal of consumer purchasing trends. Like craft beer, it doesn't really matter to most people if a product is actually artisanal, so long as it *appears* to be. Essentially, it all boils down to marketing, and which product can make the leap from the shelf into a customer's hands.

It seems that every other news clip about cannabis portrays the industry as either the Wild West, something in its infancy that should be viewed with caution—along with the requisite munchies joke, or the next big thing. In some ways, the first characterization isn't entirely incorrect, but conceptions about cannabis are almost entirely rooted in the novel aspect of the product itself. Names like *Cheeba Chew, Kandy Pens,* and *Kush Nuts* are always good for a laugh from the audience, but these products help lay the groundwork for a more mature market. Laugh if you will, but cannabis goods are coming for the alcohol industry's market share, and the *Kush Nuts* of the world may be the last ones laughing.

If we look at Colorado as a model for the future performance of cannabis in other states, about half of recreational consumers currently purchase flower when shopping in a dispensary. However, a recent study by the state, along with the University of Colorado Leeds School of Business, found that "a growing share of regulated marijuana sales are in marijuana flower alternatives, such as concentrates or edibles. In 2017, for example, more than one third (37.7

percent) of total sales were non-flower products, compared to 25.4 percent in 2015." The study continues, "Compared to the overall increase in marijuana sales of 51.6 percent from 2015 to 2017 ($996 million to $1.5 billion), concentrated product sales increased by 114 percent and infused edible sales increased by 67 percent over the same period." So, while a large portion of sales still consists of the purchase of traditional flower, the tides have consistently shifted in favor of cannabis extracts and edible products. My prediction is that cannabis flower will always have a place in the market, but that it will soon be broadly out-performed by extracts and infused products. The reasoning behind it is actually rather simple—when it comes to cannabis flower, there is a limit to innovation, and eventually that product will plateau. Infused products, however, currently enjoy a limitless ceiling for innovation. From new consumption methods, to functional enhancements at a chemical level and bio-aware delivery systems that result in more personalized effects based on the desires of the consumer, R&D teams will always be able to find new and improved ways to slice and dice cannabis and its derivatives, while consumers find new ways of using them.

On the topic of cannabis derivatives, there is an entirely new layer when it comes to the discussion of the merits of cannabis extracts. Consider this scenario: a person takes a daily medication for migraines, but it leaves them feeling groggy during the day and restless at night. Wouldn't it be a miracle if drug manufacturers could simply remove the chemical compounds from the pill that create those side effects? Imagine for a moment how much better pharmaceutical advertisements would be if they didn't end with a terrifying list of possible side effects. The ability to eliminate negative side effects has eluded the pharmaceutical industry, resulting in a surge in patients taking new and increased quantities of drugs in order to combat the downsides of their existing pharmacological regimen. Enter cannabis, and you can begin to understand why many feel cannabinoid science may one day sit alongside traditional prescriptions in various medical applications. During the extraction process, cannabinoids (the individual molecules responsible for various effects) can be stripped down, separated, and distilled into a single product. The resulting compound could be highly targeted to individual ailments, treating increasingly complex symptoms in a more refined manner. CBD, the popular, non-psychoactive compound in the plant, is being studied for use as an anti-inflammatory, which may provide relief from anxiety and aid in sleep and relaxation. Because the psychoactive THC has been removed, consumers can ingest these products without fear of spending the workday stoned out of their minds. Beyond that, products can be functionally enhanced with other compounds, creating an entirely new class of products with hyper-specific indications. The result of these innovations is a shift in the market from consumers making purchasing decisions based on strain and dominance, to effect-based end results. Because more and more people are entering a dispensary for the first time, we've seen products shift away from *indica* and *sativa,* toward those carrying labels like *sleep* and *romance.* The dispensary landscape from the early 2000s has shifted into an entirely new arena, one that's no longer a tool of the counterculture or designed with the already indoctrinated in mind, but instead caters to the novice. More than ever, consumers are interested in a soft and gentle introduction to cannabis, not in being thrust into a psychedelic dreamscape and left to fend for themselves. As with many other packaged goods, consumers are drawn toward products with innovative design, accessible packaging, and clear and concise instructions for consumption—let's call it the soccer mom effect. Like Barefoot Wines, Skinnygirl Margaritas, and White Claw Hard Seltzer, consumers are now more than ever interested in products that fit with their lifestyles.

So how does cannabis fit into that equation? The answer is a broad mix of cannabis products that remove the stigma from their perceived cultural attachments. The vast majority of consumers aren't looking for a product that will get them as high as possible (though some are, see: Jackson Tilley circa 2014), but rather a range of products that fit into their existing lifestyle and identity. Identity is perhaps *the* most important notion to consider in contemplating the future of cannabis. Most of the people I know who consume cannabis products on a regular basis do not identify as stoners. They aren't spending time in Haight-Ashbury or dropping acid at a Phish show four nights in a row. Rather, they are suburbanites looking for a restful night's sleep, students looking for ways to take the edge off without their liver paying the price, and professionals looking for a way to get a buzz on the golf course without needing to break for a piss every thirty minutes. The stoner archetype is a trite one, and one that doesn't have a place in the cannabis movement of the twenty-first century. As the idea of using cannabis products has become increasingly less stigmatized, more and more consumers are finding that the barrier to entry is lower. When dispensaries feel familiar and less like head shops, it suddenly becomes *cool*. That cool factor, the idea that cannabis isn't just for people who live in their mom's basement and play *Halo* all day, is where the magic of this industry has really begun to solidify. There has been a drastic shift in the consumer identity of cannabis purchasers, the evidence of which exists in the massive sales reported across the country. Billions of dollars of cannabis are purchased each year, and likely not by who you'd think. Some products are geared toward heavy, long-time consumers, while the majority are created with the novice in mind. This landscape exists at a particular intersection of time and space where we see a glimpse into what the future of the industry will look like: cannabis products that are as commonplace as alcohol, offered with easy access and running the gamut of tastes and personal preferences. The walls around the cannabis world are coming down, and it's the will of the customer that's driving the change.

Surely some of this must sound familiar. It's been done time and again across industries, where a novel idea takes root in small pockets before working its way into the zeitgeist. Take sparkling water, for example. Long considered little more than a mixer for a drink, it's been catapulted into the mainstream by a small Michigan company called LaCroix and the unrelenting buying power and social clout of the Buzzfeed Generation. The irony, of course, is that brands like Polar and Perrier had been selling huge amounts of seltzer for decades, but it wasn't until LaCroix became a staple of millennial culture (a quick search of the terms "LaCroix + millennial" brings up a staggering 1.3 million search results) that we saw something tried and true—seltzer—appear across the board in larger quantities than ever before. Seemingly overnight, every major beverage producer in the United States had launched their own line of sparkling water in an attempt to grab ahold of the market share. A new stream of products were created and launched as a result of consumer demand, just like the long list of cannabis products that now fill dispensary shelves, all thanks to a dramatic shift in popular culture, making something that had been around for decades, suddenly widely available and a key part of consumer conversations.

Cannabis businesses, in order to stay competitive, must not only capitalize on consumer trends, but create them. Cannabis-infused skincare is a perfect example. There is little, if any, evidence to suggest that smearing an infused lotion on the bags adorning the collective eyes of our generation offers any objective benefits, but that doesn't seem to matter. There is a *perceived* benefit in doing so, one that's rooted in "newness" and a perceived social benefit in being known as an early adopter to a new trend. Why spend $215 on La Mer under-eye cream, when you can use an artisanal, cruelty-free, single-origin, boutique, hemp serum instead? In cannabis, just like in many other verticals, there's been a shift away from price point as a marker of status, toward being viewed as a trendsetter as the ultimate form of cultural relevance. Indeed, cannabis products don't just serve the masses as a way to get high, but rather they tell a story about us as *human beings*. And what story is that, exactly? For many, an Instagram post about cannabis does more than just generate a few dozen likes. It makes a statement about our beliefs and the truths many hold to be self-evident: cannabis use carries with it an inherent statement around individualism and self-expression, manufactured by the industry as a link to years-old ideas around counter-culture and personal freedoms. The typical cannabis consumer sees herself not as someone party to old ideas about the plant, but rather as an early adopter and a breaker of social barriers. The humor in this, of course, is that modern forms of cannabis have been used for the better part of a century, and the twentysomethings buying weed from glistening, modern dispensaries, are reaping the benefits of another group's efforts forty years prior. It paints a picture of someone who feels they've cast away the tropes of generations past, and instead created a new narrative for what it means to integrate cannabis into her daily life. Cannabis has begun to emerge from the shadows, many will tell you, and its means of doing so can be distilled down to a simple idea shared throughout their online personas: #Weed.

The extraordinary rise in the popularity of cannabis is evident throughout the country, thanks in large part to the role that social media has played in destigmatizing its use. Whereas a decade ago, it would have been close to impossible to publish an op-ed or a book on the merits of cannabis, influencers and normal people alike can share their cannabis experiences with just a few clicks. With the advent of social media sites like Twitter, anyone can lift the veil and come out proudly in support of cannabis as a part of a healthy lifestyle, all in 280 characters or less. What's more, products are created increasingly with this cultural shift in mind—when something is "grammable" the likelihood of increased visibility and, by extension, sales, also goes up. With traditional means of advertising still off the table, the rise of cannabis influencers has created a marked shift in the way cannabis producers can reach potential customers. In turn, as more and more posts online are related to cannabis use, it creates a cycle of acceptance whereby users rejoice in a shared experience. If a well-known blogger posts about using CBD oil as part of their skincare regimen, it opens the door for their followers to do the same. Think of it as trickle-down canna-nomics. When those with the largest audiences bring cannabis into popular culture, it sends an immediate invitation for others to do the same. In many respects, we have social media to thank for the popularization of cannabis in the twenty-first century, and the resulting boon in product diversity can be attributed to that as well.

While $144 million a barrel may seem incomprehensible, it's merely a drop in the bucket that is the deep ocean of what mainstream cannabis sales may soon look like. One day, the stigma around cannabis will entirely disappear, and commoditization will shift the market into that of any other branded good. More than ever, consumers are seeking an identity-based item that helps solidify their own personal brand. Whether large scale or small, people are no longer just looking for a means to an end. Rather, they are attempting to strike a balance between effect and personality, a juxtaposition between what used to be and what's to come. Cannabis isn't just a tool for recreation or medicine. It's a means to carve out a role in a larger existence. In what is one of the largest and most rapid cultural shift of our lifetime, cannabis has gone from a tool of the counterculture to a must-have accessory, and we've only begun to scratch the surface. Say goodbye to the vodka-soda; say hello to cannabis and LaCroix. Who'd have thought?

CHAPTER 9

Lightbulb

It was 2016 and the VIP gifting program had turned into a full-time job. I'd been living in LA for close to two years and was finally beginning to fall into a routine. Every day, I delivered gift boxes, wrote notes, and attended events. I was doing so much networking that I felt like a walking Linkedin connection, struggling to keep my eyes open as I navigated countless introductions to strangers. Tedious as it sometimes was, I loved the simplicity of networking for business. All the cards are on the table. We shake hands, make eye contact, and share a quiet understanding that we're only exchanging pleasantries on the off chance that we might one day need favors from each other. It's selfishness disguised as polite conversation. We trade business cards and casually quip "great font!" (the same line I use no matter how great—or terrible—your card is). It goes into my pocket, and from my pocket into a desk drawer that looks like a raffle drawing for a free sub at a Midtown Quiznos. Perhaps it's the passed canapés, which plague networking events, that ultimately create the illusion of a real connection—it feels vaguely reminiscent of dinner with a friend.

During my first years in Los Angeles, I had a single standing appointment. Every Monday night, I'd make my way from Barbie's house in the hills down to West Hollywood to attend a men's AA meeting at the behest of my sponsor. At first, I hated it and could barely summon the nerve to go, namely because of the traffic (but also because of the, you know, honest discussions about my sobriety). One night, standing out on the sidewalk while smoking a cigarette, a time-honored tradition in AA, I laid eyes on the most gorgeous man I'd ever met. Dark features and blue eyes, coupled with a voice in my head that yelled, "I'm gonna marry this guy." Nervous, I spent the better part of ten minutes talking about the equine therapy program I'd done while in rehab. For those who don't know, equine therapy involves creating an image of one's emotions in the dirt using pool noodles and Christmas ornaments. Once completed, a horse will approach and clomp its hoof into the ground if it "feels you're being authentic." Michael, the blue-eyed mystery man laughed along with me at the grim fate of society if this was any indication of the types of solutions people sought in lieu of genuine emotional development. The meeting ended, and he went out the door before I had a chance to get his phone number. I spent the next two weeks scouring Instagram, in search of anyone named Michael in the greater Los Angeles area. Not an easy task, I assure you. Remember when I told you I was a busybody? Lo and behold, I found him and sent him a message. Two weeks passed and I didn't hear a word. Then, one night, a message popped up on Facebook, and it was a note from Michael asking me on a date. You see, while I was hunting Michaels on Instagram, he was hunting Jacksons on Facebook. This is the current state of dating in the millennial world. What can I tell you? One date in, and we were in love. After three months, we'd moved in together. (Spoiler alert: we got married.)

I attended that same Monday night meeting throughout my time in LA. It wrapped at around nine, at which time I would hop in my car and head to the Polo Lounge. Every week the same table, the same waiter, the same order (McCarthy salad, chopped, no eggs, dressing on the side). After the entrée, out would come a soufflé, pre-ordered with care via the fake email I'd set up to make it seem as though I was important enough to have an assistant. This was Beverly Hills after all, and if I couldn't actually *be someone*, I could at least pretend. I ate there so often, the memories blend together, with the exception of one particular night.

My phone rang and I stepped out into the hall to answer it. On the other line was my then-boss, a new recruit who, in theory, had been brought in to oversee some of our marketing. She informed me that she'd hired a (now-defunct) advertising agency to help name a new product. Coming in at a cost which I'm far too modest to reveal (damn my NDA), they returned a spreadsheet with naming ideas. Inside it, she told me, was an exact copy of synonyms for "weed" and "vape" pulled from Thesaurus.com. "You've got to be fucking kidding me." The voice on the other end of the line sounded breathless, desperate, and totally shocked. She'd dropped an absurd amount of money for these ideas, and they were totally useless. The deadline for the launch was coming up, and she was out of time. After further discussion, she told me that she'd let the agency go, and, just as some added salt to the wound, our PR consultant had announced her retirement that same week. Suddenly, we were left without anyone to handle the company's communication strategy.

"What about me?" I asked.

I don't know what came over me to be so bold as to suggest that a fresh-from-rehab twenty-four-year-old could handle PR for a company worth hundreds of millions of dollars. The words sprayed out of my mouth, a verbal spoonful of scalding miso soup.

"Yeah, what about you?" she asked flatly, after a pause.

"Yes. What about me for the job?"

Another pause.

"Hmmm…what *about you* for the job?" She was just repeating things back to me and placing the emphasis on different words. It was a twenty-first-century "Who's on First?" starring a woman in her fifties and a young man who pre-orders soufflés from a fake email account. "I'll get back to you." The phone clicked.

"What the fuck was that?" I muttered to myself at the valet stand after making a hasty exit from the restaurant, barely remembering to pay my tab. "Do I have a new job? Am I a PR professional now? Does this mean I get a company credit card? Should I get highlights?" None of the answers were evident.

I spent the next three months doing everything I could to make the case that I should be running the company's public relations efforts. It wasn't obvious to anyone, least of all myself, in what world I was qualified for the job. But I pressed on, slowly wearing down those around me in the famously exhausting *Jackson D. Tilley Method of Agitating Persuasion.*™ Call after call, text after text, I planted the seed at every opportunity, never missing a chance to promote my newly acquired skillset. Over my morning coffee, my iPhone sounded off with the distinct *ping* of a new email. I heard rumors, but assumed they weren't true. The woman on the other end of the line was no longer working for the company. Well, fuck. There was no way I was getting the job now. I'd spent three months barking up a tree that was on its way to the lumber mill. The funny thing is, I loved my job at the time and had never even considered a career in PR until that fateful night. Suddenly, though, it was an itch that I couldn't scratch. I've always joked that I wasn't put on Earth to work. That had been my mantra until the idea of being a publicist came across my empty plate at the Polo Lounge. Was this all about to crash to the ground? Now that I'd finally found what I was good at?

My phone rang and it was two of the company's partners on the line. I'd assumed, like the ball of anxiety that I am, that perhaps I, too, was getting fired. Instead, they told me to book a flight to Denver. They wanted to discuss public relations. I hung up and squealed. Michael and I headed to the airport.

In a small office at the front of company headquarters, we laid out a plan for what it would look like to bring PR in-house. Truth be told, I had no idea what I was doing, but I had grand plans that all seemed, at the very least, feasible. The owners of the company seemed to agree, and with what seemed like remarkably little discussion, they offered me the job of public relations manager. I walked out of their office, and so began my career in corporate communications.

The first few weeks were a stressful nightmare. I'd learned a fair amount about PR while in college, but years of drug use had left my memories from that time a bit…hazy. I downloaded a few books, read up on the basics, and was off to the races. With another 4/20 fast-approaching, I worked with Ann, one of my PR mentors, to try to secure some coverage for an event that we were hosting. We'd spent about a week working on a pitch for Buzzfeed, as they often provide a decent amount of coverage during cannabis events. By some miracle, my phone rang and it was the lead producer for Buzzfeed News. He'd liked our pitch and decided to come to Denver to livestream our *Art of 4/20* party to hundreds of thousands of viewers. For the event, our marketing director, Brittany, had set out to do what she always does: flawlessly elevate the brand. Beyond that, she and the rest of her team work tirelessly to steer perceptions away from dated, stoner stereotypes, instead focusing on creating high-end events that further the mission of bringing cannabis into the mainstream. Held at an old warehouse-turned-hip bar, the *Art of 4/20* created a new take on an old holiday, featuring live art installations, custom clothing, signature cocktails, and, of course, cannabis consumption. Since it's not legal in Colorado to consume cannabis inside an establishment that holds a liquor license, she rented several limousine buses and parked them in front of the venue, allowing patrons to consume both substances in peace within the confines of the law. The Buzzfeed producer arrived in Denver the day of the event. We picked him up in Ann's black Lincoln Town Car and whisked him off to the lab, where Chris Driessen eagerly awaited us. Chris gave a tour of the facilities, walking viewers through the process of making cannabis oil, and offering a brief glimpse into our world. It was my first real coup, a moment that I will never forget, because it made my understanding of *myself* crystal clear. Before this moment, I had no idea what I wanted to be when I grew up. I'd largely just assumed I would marry well and never have to work again, but that's tough to do without some prior experience at keeping a home. In that moment, with the cameras blinking, the mics taped to the chests of those around me, and the countless viewers watching from home, I was hooked. I was almost two years sober by this point, and I'd found my new drug of choice: publicity.

We're all familiar with the twenty-four-hour news cycle and its cultural byproducts. What may come as a surprise is how frequently newsworthy stories are truly just the result of a well-timed pitch or called-in favor. In large part, the news we see all around us is placed there at the behest of a frantic voice on the other end of an email chain or phone call, either trying to make the news or stay ahead of it. We're talking, of course, about publicists, and their often tumultuous relationships with members of the press.

Many of the people who work in communications are, generally speaking, horrible. Not just your run-of-the-mill nightmares, but pushy, agitating, always-asking-for-something, two-in-the-morning-emailing badgers. But what does a twenty-six-year-old know about any of this? Quite a lot, actually. Most of the news you've read about the big business in cannabis, I've placed. I talk shit about publicists because I am one. Unless a reporter from the *Wall Street Journal* has told you to go fuck yourself, have you really made it? While some lie in bed counting sheep in an attempt to fall asleep without Ambien, I lie awake counting press clippings, earned media, and pitch metrics. It's not quite a sleeping pill, but it usually does the trick. My friend Daryn Carp quips that "It's PR, not the ER." I wish it always felt like that. In my first year in the new job, I received what could only be described as a crash course in schmoozing, begging, and pleading, all in the name of securing coverage.

Along the way, I learned a few things. Hardly anyone gets into public relations because they want to be liked. In fact, to succeed, you really need to be okay with being despised by many of the people you deal with on a daily basis. The stories that get told are the ones that get pitched to the most outlets the greatest number of times. It's a pretty simple formula. I'm a fervent advocate of the free press and, in the case of cannabis, it's the best tool our industry has for changing the dialogue around being a cannabis consumer in the twenty-first century.

It requires persistence, a penchant for being annoyingly friendly, and thicker skin than you'd find on a crocodile about to be turned into a Birkin. Journalists receive thousands of emails a day, almost all of which come from a publicist pitching a piece on this year's hottest fashion accessory (spoiler alert: it's Gucci belts) or begging for a cover story about the tech world's latest IT stock. Journalists, by and large, loathe being cold-called by publicists. But we keep doing it, because we believe in our clients and we believe in the stories they want to tell. Pitching stories is a bit like dating as a millennial, and it happens in four stages:

1. *The Crush:* I've been following you on Twitter for a while now. I sometimes like your tweets, and I'm the first one to notice when you cover a story on my beat. *I want you* (to write about my client). I have the latest, greatest, *hottest* pitch, and you haven't lived until you've read it. You respond to my email and say "Would like to hear more." My heart flutters, my blood pressure rises, and I imagine a moment in the distant future where we stroll into the editorial room together and work on a story so clearly biased, so evidently without merit, that it can only be described as the fluff piece to end all fluff pieces. It's more than just a crush. I think I'm in love (with your readership numbers).

2. *The Date:* It's been about a month since we first spoke. I send you press releases. You reply back, "cool!" It's a bit one-sided, but I don't mind. As I've told you in my many emails, I've

never met someone like you—you're the only one who I want (to cover my company in a six-page inside spread with front cover lead-in). You come off as distant, but that only makes me want you more. Finally, you relent. You agree to hop on a call. My hands glisten with sweat as I think about it. "Will we use your dial-in number or mine? Are you on Eastern or Pacific time? Do you have a hard stop at ten? No problem, so do I! (See, we already have so much in common.)" Our first phone date goes well—you agree to run away with me, or at least my company's story. The article gets published, and I imagine what our future stories will look like, where they will live online, who they'll be read by, and what my life will look like knowing I've finally found the outlet of my dreams.

3. *The Breakup:* I haven't heard from you in weeks. We had one night of amazing press, and you ghosted me. I don't want to email you. I'm too proud. One thing leads to another, and after a few too many LaCroix, I give in. It's not my fault that *When Harry Met Sally* was playing on HBO. It made me miss you. It made me miss...*us.* I send you an advance copy of a press release, and you reply with a simple "Unsubscribe." Maybe it was a mistake? Maybe you didn't realize it was coming from me, your favorite publicist. I wait the standard three days and reached out again: "Just wanted to touch base. Hadn't spoken in a while, and I have a story idea I'd like to run past you." Nothing. Radio silence. Maybe I came on too strong? Maybe you found another source that was hotter than me. Maybe they gave you the kind of tip I couldn't. It was fun while it lasted, but I guess it just wasn't meant to be.

4. *The Rebound:* It's fine! I've moved on to *better* outlets. I've found an outlet who's happy to speak to my boss, even if it is Christmas Eve and their family is in town for the first time in a decade. My new source has better back-links anyway, and

they respond to my emails within a week. They think my persistence is charming—I emailed my new outlet fifteen times before getting a response, and now I'm getting a cover story out of it.

There's a blurb attributed to Bill Gates, which frequently makes the rounds online, that has the Microsoft founder claiming, "If I was down to my last dollar, I'd spend it on public relations." A lovely quote, but one that he likely never said. A quick Google search brings up 52 million results, but not a single page that actually demonstrates Bill Gates ever uttered this glowing endorsement of my profession. And yet, can you think of a better testament to the power of the publicist hive mind than an unsourced quote existing in more than 50 million places online? It's the public relations equivalent of saying, "My boyfriend goes to school in Canada. You wouldn't know him." Except, in this case, everyone believes you.

Being a publicist is rough; being a publicist in the cannabis industry is rougher. I'm talking sandpaper-on-a-sunburn rough. PR essentially boils down to one thing: take the opinions, values, and long-held beliefs of others and convince them that they're incorrect. Sounds simple enough, right? If you've ever found yourself in the comments section of a news article or on the Facebook page of that one old, racist relative you somehow haven't blocked, then you have a pretty decent idea how vehemently people will defend their beliefs. Cannabis has been demonized in the media—and society as a whole—for the better part of the last century. To act as a publicist is to act as a fixer, someone who can change the narrative as it relates to their client. In the world of cannabis PR, it's not just about pitching stories and getting coverage; it's about using the media as a tool to convince the American people that their age-old beliefs about cannabis are incorrect and that they've been fundamentally misled about the realities of the plant. Take former House Speaker John Boehner, who in 2011 stated that he was "unalterably opposed" to the legalization of marijuana. Fast forward seven years and he's sitting on the board of a major cannabis company. Prior to this change of heart, he'd consistently voted against any form of responsible cannabis reform. Apparently the grass is greener on our side.

Public relations professionals in legacy businesses don't have the same uphill climb; they simply seek coverage to keep their clients in the spotlight. I seek coverage to change the world. I'm sure you must be rolling your eyes at the notion that weed PR can have any meaningful impact on society at large; however, it's more than just working to sell products. It's battling to alter notions that the consumption of cannabis erodes the very fabric of our world. It's fighting a puritanical belief that the vices of others will be the downfall of everything we hold dear. I'm here to offer a different perspective: indeed, cannabis use *will* cause great social harm—so long as it continues on as a black-market operation without government oversight and regulation. You either support the regulated cannabis industry or you support a black market. Without a regulated market, it stands to reason that an unregulated one thrives. When left to their own devices, without a regulatory body leading the charge on oversight, the seedy underbelly of illegal cannabis sales can grow and develop. If that's what you favor, you must realize the human costs when enthusiasts are forced to buy cannabis from drug dealers. In 2017 alone, close to 25,000 people were murdered as a direct result of cartels in and around the US-Mexico border. These are the realities forced upon humanity when reasonable drug regulations are not created, so I will say it again for the people in the back: if you don't support regulated cannabis, you support the black market and the human costs associated with its survival. Cartels in Mexico generate between $20 billion and $29 billion annually as a direct result of selling drugs across the border and into the United States. Since 2006, more than 150,000 people, many of them civilians, have been murdered as a result of the cartels' drug war. I'm not saying that federal legalization of cannabis will put an immediate halt to international drug wars, but it would certainly lessen its human and economic costs by eliminating one of the cartels' revenue streams: black market cannabis.

The novelty of cannabis PR is twofold: you're trying to pitch a product *and* change an old narrative. Running communications for finance companies, restaurants, or any other goods or services that benefit from a strong PR effort often entails pitching the same old stories. Cannabis offers a unique angle. When I first started working in the space, journalists were being pitched cannabis stories for the first time. While I'm sending out emails with headlines like, "This cannabis company will pay you to sample weed!" and "Meet the industry power players who want to bring marijuana into retailers across the country," some of my PR colleagues in other industries aren't as fortunate. One friend battles to defuse the "clean wind energy kills eagles" narrative from President Trump, while another struggles to find a way to make a new type of three-hole punch seem interesting. The corporate cannabis industry is a new one, and thus has long been devoid of the more traditional pillars of a standard business. As a result, many in the space are just now getting around to hiring someone to handle their communications efforts, and the resulting conversations across the industry are elevated as a result. In a few short months, I'd gone from being the most popular guy in the room—the one who delivers gift boxes filled with goodies, to one of the least popular—the guy who harasses you at all hours of the night wondering when a story will run.

The transition from celebrity gifting to PR wasn't necessarily an easy one, but it was one that made sense. I'd spent an inordinate amount of time building relationships before I finally realized that the *building of relationships* was my greatest strength. Gifting and PR are similar in many ways, namely that it's all about building rapport with people in positions of power. In lieu of gift boxes I now send pitches, but the schmoozing done in years past has paid off. Now, with iPhone in hand, I can make a call, ask for a favor, and see our name in print the next day. In the grand scheme of things it's small, but to me it feels like power.

INTERVIEW WITH PETER MILLER AND BILLY LEVY

SLANG Worldwide cofounder and CEO Peter Miller is an experienced entrepreneur with ten years of executive experience. He and Billy Levy co-founded Mettrum Health Corp., a leading Canadian-licensed producer that was acquired by Canopy Growth. Billy Levy, president of SLANG Worldwide, co-founded Virgin Gaming along with Sir Richard Branson, and advised on the creation of Virgin Mega. I first met Peter and Billy two years ago and was instantly struck by their ability to articulate both sides of the argument around cannabis as an investment. Here, we speak about that same topic.

Ten years ago, I tell you that you're going to be taking a cannabis company public in Canada. What's your reaction?

PM: Ten years ago, Billy and I were discussing the financial apocalypse over weekly turkey burgers and plotting the entrepreneurial schemes that would best thrive in that environment. A cannabis business would have been *perfect* back then, but legal cannabis, let alone scaled, commercial, legal cannabis was the *furthest* thing from my mind. Billy was building an online gaming platform that was the precursor to what we know as "e-sports" today, and I was hustling commercial media production work while going to business school. As twentysomethings, though, we understood the consumer appeal and recognized the market opportunity. It wasn't until Colorado's ballot initiative to legalize adult use cannabis in 2012 that the wheels really started turning in my head about this as a viable business opportunity.

BL: I'd like some of whatever you're smoking.

In what ways did your previous experience prepare you for working in cannabis?

PM: I worked with artists and performers earlier in my career. Some of those artists' behaviors and attitudes are shockingly similar to a lot of cannabis growers I've dealt with. I say that with all respect, as both groups just want to achieve greatness at any cost, but trying to keep the trains running on time in that environment requires extreme diplomacy, patience, and creativity...luckily we buy most of our material wholesale at SLANG now and we can focus on the myriad other challenges in getting product to market. All of the life and professional experience you can bring to the industry is great, but nothing prepares you for the rollercoaster that is the

107

cannabis industry. After six years at it, my mind is blown by something new every day.

BL: One of my previous businesses, Virgin Gaming, operated in the online gaming space and was subject to online gambling regulations. We were not technically considered online gambling in the US, and fell under "skilled gaming" laws. Skilled gaming is regulated on a state-by-state basis, different in many states, and only legal in thirty-nine of them. So the whole experience of building a business that complied with state legislation across the country has for sure been helpful, as there are many parallels to the cannabis industry. Aside from that, every day is a new challenge and adventure—I use what I know and have experienced, which is helpful, but we're doing a lot of things for the first time, which is awesome!

What does the future of the cannabis space look like?

PM: It looks like an extremely high growth and exciting category within consumer packaged goods (CPG), following the commercial and economic conventions of CPG. The social stigma will be significantly lower, inviting more consumers to enjoy the product and have great experiences with cannabis. The best brands, built on the best products, distributed most broadly will win in that environment.

BL: Brands, brands, brands. Consumers are experiencing cannabis in new form factors (vapes, edibles, the list goes on) and developing relationships with the brands that deliver them the experience they're enjoying. Those relationships being defined now will last lifetimes.

How far out are we from US federal legalization?

PM: Yikes...closer than we were yesterday, but probably further than many think. I don't think we can or should take anything for granted. Bill Maher had a great segment on legalization in February 2016 that still resonates. He reminded the audience of other rights that have been rolled back... since 1991, 81 percent of abortion clinics in America have closed down. He emphasized that "legalizing pot is a long way from a done deal." That said, I'm a born optimist, and also believe in the power of economic incentives. I've joked before that the most addictive drug in the world is tax revenue, and the tax revenue generated by state-level legalization is the gateway drug to federal legalization. We'll see.

BL: In my mind, I hope it doesn't happen too fast. The fragmented nature of different laws rolling out state by state has given us a competitive advantage, as we get to learn and scale as markets develop, while many established business institutions from other industries sit on the sidelines, because they're nervous about the law. It's a unique situation that's created opportunities for teams like ours. We will continue to build and grow, adapting with legalization laws along the way, so honestly I don't spend too much time thinking about it.

If and when that day comes, what lessons can the United States market learn from the Canadian one?

PM: Let the free market determine who wins, loses, and at what scale! Don't over-regulate anything, but maintain strict rules that protect consumer health and safety. I think the Colorado model is a pretty good one, and the "legalization experiment" in that state has worked extremely well on all fronts. Counterintuitively, I think Canada has more to learn from America about good cannabis regulation than it has to teach.

Have you always been interested in cannabis (as a business!), or is it a recent development?

PM: At Thanksgiving in 2012, my wife's cousin told me about the designated grower (caretaker) model that Canada created years earlier to help patients access medicine. It sounded awesome, but a bit sketchy and untenable from an oversight standpoint, as it had scaled to include thousands of participants. The next day, I looked into the laws. Coincidentally, the government had just issued guidance that they were replacing that old medical program with the world's first federally legal, regulated commercial market for medical cannabis. All of my entrepreneurial sensors started going off at once, and I haven't looked back since.

BL: I've been enjoying cannabis since I was a teenager, but never thought of it as a business as it was unfathomable to do so for most of our lives. Peter got me interested in the business opportunity in 2013 and we haven't looked back. This is one of the greatest opportunities in the history of capitalism, and is going to be one of the fastest growing global consumer trends for the foreseeable future.... I couldn't imagine wanting to do anything else.

In what way has the media impacted the changing perceptions of cannabis?

PM: From *Reefer Madness* to the SLANG IPO being covered by mainstream media outlets, and from Just Say No to O.pen ads on the airport security trays in California, I'd say the perception shift has been palpable. The media has played a major part. It's still perplexing to see cannabis social media accounts getting shut down while all manner of hate speech and violent content goes unchecked. But like I said about legalization not being a done deal, we can't take for granted that the stigma will disappear by itself and the perception will change without continued advocacy, diplomacy, and leadership by de facto industry representatives. We have to be good citizens, not blindly espouse the benefits of cannabis without having honest conversations about the risks of overuse, and generally encourage open dialogue and the normalization of responsible cannabis use.

BL: Cannabis has been stigmatized for so long as an illegal substance and all the media coverage is now creating awareness that is driving social acceptance. Cannabis is now constantly in the news from financial to consumer press and it's helping to normalize as people are getting more educated on all the benefits of the products and opportunities to participate in the industry. With all the marketing regulations, the media is important to help tell our stories and get the word out too!

In 2019, what does a cannabis consumer look like? How does that consumer compare with that of, say, 2000? 2010?

PM: I think Billy is entirely right. Acceptance has led to openness about use and changed our collective perception of what a cannabis consumer looks like. Other than form factor, I don't think the consumer behavior, behind the scenes, has changed too much. I bet that if you tested the collective waste treatment facilities of the western world, the THC per capita in the urine would be shockingly similar from rural to urban areas and across all socio-economic and political strata. We should look into that. Somebody likely already has that data, though, and I expect a meta study is more appealing to our data team than going to do that primary research!

BL: The perception has changed more than the consumer, as it's now more mainstream and acceptable. New form factors like vapes and edibles, as well as laws legalizing in specific locations have brought cannabis consumers back to the plant. They can use now without breaking the law, *but* people have been using cannabis forever and will now just do it more frequently and in different ways.

What would you say is the most misunderstood aspect of this industry?

PM: The most dangerous thing about cannabis is investing in it, and the biggest myth about growing cannabis is that it's a good way to make money!

BL: It's easy money. Lots of people get into it and think they're just going to strike it rich without considering the amount of work, patience, and persistence that's required to be successful.

CHAPTER 10

The Fox in the Living Room

"There's a fucking fox in the living room."

Michael and I were now both working at the same company, and we'd been given the master suite at a house rented for the company retreat in the mountains. When we first walked in the front door, we were both highly skeptical of why we'd been given the largest room, when some twenty-five of us, including the owners, were attending. We surveyed the room, looking for some evidence of a prank, but nothing was found. It also bears mentioning that not only was I working side by side with my fiancé, but also with my best friend from college, Brittany, and her boyfriend, Weston, who was *also* one of my best friends and a member of our elite (at least in our minds) dorm-room gang known as the Buckingham Yacht Club. We'd met in the dorms during our first semester of college, and over the years had only grown closer. Since 2010, we'd smoked an unquantifiable amount of weed and had also somehow found a way to work together and bolster our professional success. Some people call us nuts, but I can't think of a better job than one that feels like a continuation of college, with the bulk of the crew all in place. Our company is unique insofar as there are about five couples who work together in the same office, yet never seem to argue. The company was even co-founded by a husband and wife duo, Jeremy and Amanda, who sort of set the stage for the rest of us. There are many companies out there who purport to operate more like a family than a business, but I'm hard pressed to think of any that take it as seriously as the team at Organa Brands. If you doubt me, when's the last time you went on a vacation with all of your colleagues, *and actually enjoyed it?* (That's what I thought.) For us, there isn't work without play, so we try to blend the two together at any opportunity.

The company trip was in full swing, our bags were unpacked, and we went downstairs to join the festivities. It was a cool Friday night in Breckenridge, a small ski town two hours outside of Denver. We'd been beckoned to the mountain compound to kick off what would eventually become a mainstay of our business: a leadership retreat. In the kitchen, the then-president of our US operations, Chris Driessen, was preparing shishito peppers with goat cheese, a bougie staple of 2017 cuisine. Chris is a riddle wrapped in an enigma wrapped in bacon: a good ol' boy from Texas, he simultaneously loves fine wine, Texas football, truffle salt, barbecue, his Range Rover, and, of course, weed. He's at times both genteel and crude, well mannered and gruff. Gathered around the massive marble island, colleagues shared drinks and stories. One of the cofounders, Jeremy, raised a glass to make a toast. "It's been an incredible year, and we have some big news. We've decided to sell the company." There was a long pause. A pall came over the group as if we'd just collectively seen our parents naked. People stood and anxiously crossed their arms, waiting with bated breath to hear what would become of us. Would we keep our jobs? Would we get replaced with the new owner's teams? What would happen to our office, our benefits, our perks? My hands went clammy as I stood motionless.

"Nah, I'm just fucking with you. Let's eat!" That's Jeremy in a nutshell. He's a disruptor in every sense of the word. Not just in the traditional form—someone who finds new ways of doing business—but someone who finds immense joy in flipping things on their heads. I often describe him as the most misunderstood man in the world: someone who loves elaborate pranks, picking political fights on Facebook, and watching people's reactions as they find out he's just played a well-orchestrated joke on them. But below the surface, he's incredibly giving and fiercely loyal. He is the type of entrepreneur who simultaneously makes adversaries laugh and tremble, while somehow managing to be right about 99.9 percent of the things he goes to bat for (don't tell him I admitted that).

To be disruptive in this industry, a person has to wear many hats and hold several conflicting ideals to be true. Just like loving both $200 Napa wine and a six-dollar fast-food BBQ platter, to survive in the world of cannabis, a person needs to live both inside and outside of the cannabis counterculture. With deep anti-establishment and anti-capitalist roots, how can lifelong marijuana lovers also root for big business and government regulation? In a nutshell, to survive, you must adapt. Cannabis has changed, and it's no longer just a small pleasure for the few, but a booming industry for the many. As of late 2018, there were dozens of cannabis companies traded on Canadian stock exchanges, and one behemoth in particular, Canopy Growth, which is traded on the NYSE. A far cry from a few plants being grown in a hall closet and sold in dime bags on the corner, cannabis of the twenty-first century is a grown-up business. Not fully matured, but growing faster than a Russian athlete a month away from the Olympics.

The following morning, I walked downstairs from our bedroom, and saw the fox standing in the living room. I hadn't even had my morning coffee. The house looked more like a wildlife preserve than a vacation rental. All the doors were ajar, cold air whipping through the rooms, making it all feel like a giant walk-in freezer. In the doorway, a small red fox was eating a piece of steak out of Jeremy's palm, while several onlookers grabbed photos and videos to share, as no one would believe it unless they saw it with their own two eyes. He'd lured a fox into the living room without pause or consideration.

In that moment, it occurred to me that cannabis businesses are the fox, relying more on cunning than on brute strength. By almost every measure, our industry can be out-spent, out-litigated, and out-marketed by our counterparts in other regulated industries like alcohol and tobacco. Nevertheless, relying on diligence, focus, and artful attention to our craft, the industry has blossomed into a multi-billion dollar enterprise, tackling business and regulatory issues unfathomable to most others. And like the fox, we're often regarded as a cute distraction, something to be observed, not touched. But under the right circumstances, the fox is a cerebral predator capable of wiping out a chicken coop without hesitation.

As the small creature continued to nibble bits of steak from Jeremy's palm, I suddenly realized that you need to be a little bit insane to do what we do for a living. You have to be fearless as well. I'm not saying that a willingness to feed a wild animal is the sole requirement for making it in this business, but the idea that you're willing to take risks, even if there's no immediate prize aside from being able to say you did it, speaks to the nature of the types of leaders that make up our new industry. Risk takers, adventure capitalists, thrill seekers, and innovators are just a few of the words that come to mind.

We work diligently each day to bring disruption to the world around us. When you read it in black and white, it sounds almost menacing, but the reality is quite the opposite. Cannabis, like many other vices, has long been villainized by those who simply don't understand it. I know this because I was one of those people. Sobbing to my mother about finding a bong in my brother's room ranks at the top of my list of most embarrassing memories, but only because I now see recreational cannabis use for what it is: a hobby. Like golf, going to the movies, or building puzzles, using cannabis doesn't make you interesting. It doesn't alter your personal narrative.

It doesn't add to or detract from your personal brand—it simply is. It's something people do for fun, it's something people do out of boredom, or perhaps it's just something people do when it's in front of them. Others still find immense medicinal benefits, helping with anxiety or insomnia or other symptoms from a long list of ailments. The reality is, in the same way that popping a Claritin when I have to be in the same room as a cat doesn't alter the fundamental truth about me as a person, cannabis use doesn't either. To say that the world has changed when it comes to this plant is an understatement. The world hasn't just changed; it's forgotten what it used to be like. While there are some parts of the country where marijuana use is still very much taboo, I'd say we've made a 170-degree shift from the days of *Reefer Madness*. But we're getting closer to that U-turn, and you have cannabis capitalists to thank for it.

Our company is known for its *workations*, a term used to describe a trip that could reasonably be described as business-related, even perhaps if not in the most traditional sense. We've been lucky to travel all over the world with friends who also happen to be our bosses. We've moved cross-country more than once, even to tropical islands (we'll get to that later). This trip to the mountains, though, was different. It was one of the first times such a large swath of the company had been brought together to work not *in* the business but *on* the business. We were broken into teams and spent two days working one-on-one with company ownership to discuss how our individual roles would contribute to the success of the company. For a person like me with a level of vanity and ego that would make even Madonna uneasy, it was a blissful moment to hear that I played some role in our overall success. By this point I had been made director of public relations, the first time our company had created such a position, and I was congratulated on the press we'd received in the year prior. Some months prior, I got the first big feather in my cap, landing a coveted profile in *Forbes*. After weeks of preparation, travel arrangements, media coaching, and grooming, the day arrived. Debra Borchardt, then a writer for *Forbes* and now the founder of the cannabis media platform Green Market Report, had flown out to Denver at my request. We spent two days with her, talking about the company and our plans for the future. I hate to stroke my own ego, but…it went off without a hitch. In my short career in public relations, I'd managed to accomplish something that's out of the grasp of many, and the resulting article bolstered my confidence and paved the way for me to rise up the ranks into the position I hold to this day. About a week later, I got an email with the link to the story. The headline is burned into my memory: *Meet Organa Brands, The Company that Wants to Dominate the US Cannabis Market.* Some 25,000 people had already read the story as I quickly emailed it out to the entire company.

For me, it was about more than just a story placement, it was a signal that mainstream media was growing increasingly comfortable with the idea of cannabis. That year, we went on to have our best press record in company history, increasing the number of stories about the company almost 300 percent, and it was thanks in large part to that *Forbes* article. Later on during the retreat, I sat on the couch with Chris Driessen and spoke about the future of the company. It was the first time I'd heard mention of a phrase all young people want to hear: "going public." It would turn out to be some time away, but it lit a fire inside the hearts and minds of every employee under that roof. Suddenly, we each knew that we had a larger role, a raised bar for what was going to be asked of us, and it would be critical to taking the company to its next level. I'm the first to admit that I've drunk the Organa Brands Kool-Aid. I'm in 100 percent. There has never been a single moment since that fateful day when I've doubted not only what we are doing as a company, but *why* we are doing it. While Chris Driessen gave a stump speech to the room, another of the company's cofounders, Chris McElvany, quipped to me, "Jackson, the things you're doing now will end up in textbooks one day." I was speechless, because as absurd as it sounded, I had a hunch that he might be right.

The things that happen within the walls of our business are happening for the first time in history. It's a shame that Sarah Palin ruined the word "maverick" for all of us, because that's the only way to describe the leaders of our humble company. Not only did they carve a path for the rest of the industry, but they inspired a group of young people to come together and forever alter the course of the industry in this country and beyond. Our collective goal, of course, is one shared by many red-blooded Americans—to make money. But it's more than that. The real catalyst for all we do boils down to a simple concept: create a new industry, build an amazing brand, and take it global. I guess maybe it's not so simple, but it sometimes feels that way when you're in the thick of it.

By the time the retreat ended, we'd all walked away with a new and unified vision not just for the future of the company, but for ourselves. I don't know many people outside of the nonprofit world who feel truly inspired by their work, and I think that's due in large part to the fact that most jobs are *really fucking boring*. I stared up at the ceiling from the comfort of one of those Japanese massage chairs that had been placed inside our mountain home. The trip was winding down, and my head was spinning with the thought of all the opportunities that lay before us. I'm only twenty-seven years old, but in my short life, I've been lucky enough to have three spiritual awakenings. The first, at age sixteen, when I discovered LimeWire and the resulting porn and computer viruses that went along with it. The second, at age twenty-three, when I found myself in rehab and admitted that I was a drug addict, through some miraculous twist of fate that took me from the top of a building to the bottom of a depression, back to the top of a spiritual life. And the third, which happened just two years ago, at age twenty-five, when I piled onto couches in the living room of a rented house in the mountains. I'd stumbled ass backwards into this job, relying on no skills of note, aside from an unreasonable ability to make people like me. In just a few short years, I'd gone from a drug addict intern with no idea what I wanted to do, to the director of public relations for the largest cannabis company in America. When you say it like that, it sounds like it was just a steady uphill climb, but the reality is that I tripped and clawed and cried my way forward, reaching for a prize I didn't even know existed. In three short days in the mountains, I'd somehow found my higher calling. Sure, go ahead and scoff. I'm sure you must be thinking, "Listen to this hack. He thinks he was put on this earth to spin stories and write press releases." Well, actually, I think I was.

It had only been a year since I'd switched roles from VIP gifting to a life in the world of corporate communications, but every step along the way seemed to come together in perfect harmony to get me closer to the finish line. I had always possessed an innate ability to get people to do what I wanted, and it had manifested itself in many different ways throughout the years. While an active drug addict, it looked closer to manipulation, getting my parents (bless them) to continue giving me money without asking too many questions. After I got sober, I'd managed to turn these character defects into assets that propelled my career and my life onto the next plane. The great irony of all of this is that the difference between being manipulative and being a people person, is working in public relations. I'd learned over the years a very unique set of skills: get people to like me, create value in our relationship by offering something that no one else can, and in turn have a mutually beneficial rapport that, like rising tides, raises all ships. My life had transformed from working hard to get things for *me,* to working hard to get things that benefit others (and if it happens to help me too, amazing).

I can think of no better example than this: As we were having our final meeting of the trip, I cornered a few of the executives to try to get a firm answer on a project that had been cooked up by Brittany and me. We'd hatched an insane idea for a viral marketing campaign, and we were working diligently to get it across the finish line. It would require the ownership team to sign off on an invoice that was higher than any other marketing expense we'd ever incurred, but I was absolutely certain it would be one of our most successful ventures. I spent the better part of an hour making my pitch, asking them to trust me, and then…voilà, they agreed and after quick perusal from our general counsel, the deal was signed. What would follow would eventually become one of the most successful campaigns in the history of the regulated cannabis market, and would forever alter the course of my life as a PR professional. It brought press, adoration, disdain, award nominations, piles of paperwork, news crews, paid actors, plastic bins, overseas printing facilities, and curious calls from reporters all over the country.

And it all happened in an airport.

CHAPTER 11

Relating to the Public

"Every now and then, the culture experiences a watershed, a moment when we look up and say, wow, things really have changed...I am talking about cannabis. On New Year's Day 2018, California enters a new era for legalization, which may hasten the end of decades of prohibition that have propelled a black market, ruined countless lives and obstructed research into what may be one of humanity's most helpful therapeutic substances.

"How do I know this moment of transformation is upon us? Because Friday morning, I went through a Transportation Security Administration checkpoint at Ontario International Airport and saw it with my own eyes. A sticker that covered the bottom of the tray for my belongings said in huge block letters: 'CANNABIS IS LEGAL.' There was some fine print near the bottom: 'Traveling with it is not. Leave it in California.' And beneath that admonition, there were five corporate logos, all belonging to Organa Brands, the 7-year-old cannabis company that came up with this unusual campaign."

—ROBIN ABCARIAN, *Los Angeles Times*

It's not often that a person goes toe-to-toe with the TSA. Well, that is, except for all of the times where I'm literally getting my toes stepped on during a particularly handsy pat-down. This interaction was different, though. I'd just gotten off the phone with Debra, the writer at *Forbes*. She told me that she'd just walked away from a terse phone call with the communications director at the Transportation Security Administration. *They were pissed.* The only thing that government agents hate more than public embarrassment is private harassment. Apparently, the director's phone had been ringing nonstop since news broke about our company's new advertising campaign inside the security trays in a Southern California airport. I'd been prepared for this kind of pushback. It's all part of the public relations game. No matter how hard you try, someone will always be unhappy, but a good publicist can manage the fallout ahead of time. Such was the case with Organa Brands and the TSA.

We'd spent the last six months negotiating with local airports and TSA offices in Southern California to make arrangements to run a "unique" advertising campaign. Marijuana was about to be made legal for adult use in California, and I saw the opportunity for us to really make a splash. Cannabis companies are severely restricted in terms of where they can advertise. And because advertising expenses aren't tax deductible, businesses think long and hard about where to allocate those dollars. We'd located a company that owns the patent on advertising inside of security trays at TSA checkpoints, and had been working alongside them to get approval on our campaign. The thought that a company can *patent* the concept of placing a sticker on a plastic tray is absolutely fascinating. Somehow, this media company had managed to do it. (To their patent attorney: if you're reading this, call me!) The TSA apparently found it infuriating, and later sued to nullify the patent. They lost the suit, and so it stands that if you want to run an ad inside of a security tray, there's only one company to go through.

We'd gone back and forth over the summer about how the copy would read. The initial ad that had been approved by an airport in Oakland read "Cannabis is illegal!" in all caps. Not really the message that we were trying to send. We went back and forth with several other airports until finally finding one friendly enough to allow us to stick with our mutually agreed upon language:

CANNABIS IS LEGAL
Traveling with it is not. Leave it in California.

The logos of all five of our brands appeared below the copy. Anyone who works in social media or public relations will tell you that there's no surefire way to make something go viral. It's a goal for which many strive but few achieve. There are simply too many factors at play to isolate the one thing that causes something to gain traction, but something told me that this was going to be huge.

Finally, we signed the contract and the trays went into production for an October 1 launch. In the weeks leading up to the date, I'd secured stories with major outlets, including *Newsweek*, the *LA Times*, and the *Hill*. They broke the news simultaneously, and within a few moments of the stories going live, my inbox was filled with requests from additional media to cover the story. We'd had the good sense to send camera crews and actors into the airport the week before to film the trays in use. We edited the B-roll into news clips and distributed them to outlets alongside studio photographs of the trays. The easier you can make a journalist's life, the more likely they are to cover your story. It turned out to be the perfect storm—a catchy campaign combined with strong news coverage and images fit for Instagram. We went viral. The campaign generated $4 million in ad spend equivalency (a term used in the PR world to equate the monetary value of earned media) and was picked up by thousands of news outlets, generating tens of millions of impressions for our company.

What was the point of all of it? Of course, we were thrilled to have shone the spotlight on our business, and overjoyed with how well the campaign was received by the media. If the comments section of an online video or article is any indication of public perception (hint: it isn't) then the campaign was an instant hit among those watching the story develop.

The *true* goal however, was showing the world that cannabis deserves a seat at the table. We've been cast out of the big leagues for too long. Consequently, we have a keen sense of how to do things differently. The reality is, legacy businesses can't think the same way that we do and so they work in a way that makes sense for them. If it's not broken, there's nothing to fix. That's not to say that there isn't an enormous amount of innovation in advertising taking place among the Cokes and Pepsis of the world, but for them, the media-buying landscape is unrecognizable when compared to that of the cannabis industry, who has been relegated to buying billboards and vinyl car wraps to get the word out about their product. Neither large-circulation magazines nor newspapers will print cannabis ads. In early 2019, CBS refused to run a cannabis ad during the Super Bowl. We sell a product that requires a laser-sharp focus on reaching the masses via new media, meaning we have to look outside traditional channels to execute our advertising strategies. We aim to change the way the world sees cannabis products and cannabis consumers.

I received a call from our partners on the campaign letting me know that the TSA had issued a mandate to pull the trays from circulation. Seven days in, and they'd gotten cold feet. It didn't come as a huge surprise. I was shocked they'd allowed the trays in the first place. The administration cited an obscure rule that no advertisements inside the checkpoint could cause a disturbance or it would be grounds for removal. I suppose that since our ultimate goal was to disrupt the market, we were doomed from the start. Nevertheless, didn't an agency tasked with protecting travelers have anything better to do? Or were they simply tired of receiving calls from the media asking if they condoned the use of cannabis? At the height of the campaign, headlines read "TSA launches first in-airport cannabis campaign." No wonder they were angry—we'd unintentionally made a mockery of them in national publications. (If anyone from the TSA happens to be reading this, *please* don't revoke my Pre-Check status...I can't go back to taking my shoes off.) Cancelling the campaign didn't change the astonishing fact that for one week, a federal agency had not just allowed, but *expressly approved* a cannabis business to run advertisements in an airport. It was more than just an advertising campaign, it was a signal that the cannabis world was changing.

PR is often opaque, which is very much by design. There's a sense of mystery and idealism on the part of most readers, who have little clue how a story finds its way into the pages of their local paper. It's the duty of the press to tell honest stories that inform opinions and educate the populace. It's the job of a publicist to represent their clients in the most effective way, and ensure that the media has a kind outlook on them. Of course, both of these ideas are little more than legend at this point in history, as we've all seen the kind of slant that exists across some news outlets. The cannabis industry has seen a slew of press, both good and bad, in the last decade. They say that there's no such thing as bad publicity and, in this instance, I couldn't agree more. In late 2018, the *New York Post* published a piece titled "These Are All the Ways Cannabis is Bad For You." It was a hit piece. It painted a picture of cannabis as a gateway drug, as the Reagan-era boogie man hiding in the bushes, ready to attack The Children™. How could this be good for the industry? It's simple: a mainstream publication is talking about cannabis. Even though they had many facts wrong and painted the industry in a negative light, they were promoting a dialogue around cannabis prohibition. The more we see articles, good or bad, about cannabis regulation in the press, the less time the industry finds itself living on the fringes of society. While not all of the coverage holds an enlightened view of the industry, it does promote further discussion of the issues at hand.

Marshall McLuhan famously argued that "the medium is the message." In the case of the TSA campaign, the message itself was less important than how it was being covered in the mainstream press. The manner in which we receive information is far more important than the words themselves, which is also the case in the conversation around cannabis. Twenty years ago, it would have been unheard of to read a story in the mainstream press that painted cannabis in a positive light. Now, for the most part, the media slants more and more in our favor. Science has begun to shed light on the notion that this long-demonized plant holds immense power and can offer relief to those who need it most. When we talk about messaging in the cannabis space, what we're really talking about is correcting misinformation. In 1986, the now infamous "Just Say No" campaign echoed across the airwaves. In it, Nancy Reagan made a plea to the American people, "Life can be great, but not when you can't see it. So, open your eyes to life: to see it in the vivid colors that God gave us as a precious gift to His children, to enjoy life to the fullest, and to make it count. Say yes to your life. And when it comes to drugs and alcohol, just say *no*." In some respects, she wasn't wrong. America was, as it is now, experiencing an enormous crisis with regards to drug abuse. Where she and her husband were misguided, however, was on the idea that cannabis use was at the heart of the problem. President Reagan made his stance on cannabis clear, saying "Marijuana…is probably the most dangerous drug in America today…" The cannabis industry hasn't sunk to this level of mass misinformation, but rather has risen above it and continues to Just Say No to Propaganda. There is no question that America is facing a drug epidemic, but it's not a cannabis problem. It's a prescription drug problem, and it's killing us. I know this, because it almost killed me.

I'd decided about six months before I got sober that I didn't have a pill problem. I had a depression problem. My energy was always low, and I couldn't seem to keep my eyes open during the day. It never occurred to me that dry-swallowing a fistful of benzos on a regular basis may have been the root of my problems, but as they say, hindsight is 20/20. Me? A drug addict? It simply wasn't an idea I was willing to entertain. Unlike many, I didn't go broke as a drug addict—I had great insurance. Instead of heading into an alley to buy a small baggie of pills, I made my way to the local CVS and picked up my monthly dose. For two years, I was receiving 180 tablets a month of Xanax, little round pills that seemed to be the only thing to quiet my nerves. They call them "mommy's little helper" for a reason. I was also filling prescriptions for 180 capsules of Ritalin, a classic in the world of ADHD treatment. Add on top of that 30 Ambien, 30 Prozac, and some vitamin E for good measure, and I was a veritable walking advertisement for the idea of better living through science. Something to wake me up, something to calm me down, and something to make me happy. That's more than 300 pills a month, happily provided by my local pharmacist, and all prescribed to me by my treating physician. I was not the exception in the epidemic of over-prescription that plagues our country; I was the rule. This is the current state of medicine in America.

We're one of only two countries in the world that allow pharmaceuticals to be advertised on television. As a result, people walk into their doctor's offices and ask for drugs by name. I was first prescribed Xanax and Ritalin my freshman year of college, during a particularly challenging time. Like many others, I trusted my doctor to know what was best for my health. She pulled out her prescription pad and did what many physicians are trained to do with mental health issues—treat the symptoms, not the cause. (Let me also state for the record that I don't blame my doctor for my drug problem. Addiction is, in my view, almost certainly genetic, and if it wasn't prescription drugs, it would've been something else.) Americans are addicted to more than just pills. We're addicted to the notion that there's a cure-all for our health problems. When I have strep throat, I take a Z-Pak (a pharmaceutical cocktail that's the antibiotic equivalent of a nuclear bomb), and I get better. It's not complicated: when we have a medical problem, medicine is often the only solution. However, when we begin to treat issues arising from our own circumstances—happiness, agency, "not fitting in"—with prescription drugs, that's an entirely different animal. And that's when many of us turn to prescription drugs looking for an answer, for an escape from our own reality.

In a perfect storm of ready access to prescription drugs and a mental-health crisis, we see opioid overdoses killing more Americans than breast cancer. No one should argue that all drug use has negative consequences. For some, the end result of cannabis use is relief after a lifetime of pain caused by seizures. For others, their grades take a dip because they're more interested in getting stoned than going to class. It's Newton's third law, every action in life is met with some sort of equal and opposite reaction. Cannabis is a powerful form of medicine for many, and a welcome respite from hangovers for others who've switched from Bud Light to Banana Kush. But, as with all drugs, we must use them responsibly. As is the case with *any* prescription drug, there is a way to consume responsibly, and there is a way to abuse.

Despite its listing as a schedule one substance, which requires it has *zero* medical use and carries a high likelihood for abuse, there is little science to back up the notion that cannabis is physically addictive. Drugs like fentanyl, on the other hand, are one of the leading causes of overdose deaths in America. Yet the DEA classifies it as a schedule two substance, meaning that while it does have the potential for abuse, it offers medical benefits that outweigh its risk. For the skeptics, I beg you to look at these two drugs side by side and tell me which one has the highest likelihood of causing harm. We've all heard it before—no one has ever died of a cannabis overdose. The worst, and I mean *the worst*, a person may experience as a result of consuming too much cannabis is heart palpitations, nausea, and paranoia. But you won't die, at least not from an overdose. Now, the cannabis of 2018 is drastically more potent than that which was around in the 1970s, but lethal it is not. There are, of course, cases of impaired driving resulting in death, but as of now, there's never been a case of a cannabis overdose resulting in death.

Prescription drugs, on the other hand, kill people every day. The *New York Times* recently published a horrifying story about synthetic opioids like fentanyl. Overdoses from that category of drugs have risen 540 percent in the last three years, from 3,000 to 20,000. Drug overdoses now kill Americans at a faster rate than the HIV epidemic did *at its peak.*

I'm sure you're thinking, I thought we were supposed to be talking about the power of the public relations? Well, we are. In a period of American history plagued by misinformation about drug abuse and the problems that stem from it, our greatest asset is the media. War-on-drugs era propaganda is a noxious weed. Clear and accurate information about the risks and benefits of cannabis consumption is the only way to rip it from the ground. Nothing in this world exists in a vacuum, and so it's impossible to talk about cannabis without talking about other drugs. Where the distinction lies is that cannabis hasn't yet had a fighting chance to make its case in the public eye. Because of strict government regulation, there are few, if any, large scale studies on the health benefits of cannabis. We know, anecdotally, that it offers profound benefits for those who need it, and can often serve as not a gateway drug, but rather as a so-called exit drug for people trying to wean themselves off of prescription drugs. I don't claim to know any of this as scientific fact because I'm not a scientist. Nor am I a doctor. What I am is a publicist, and my job is to tell stories for others. It's my duty to tell the story of the cannabis industry, to encourage further research and help to solidify long-term access to this plant that is both consistent and safe. If we hope to see a nationwide regulated market and put an end to the the imprisonment of nonviolent drug offenders, we are obligated to force the issue into mainstream discussion. A regulated market is a safe one, and accurate reporting and access to accurate information is our only path to getting there.

Like the ad campaign in the TSA trays, the goal isn't to just shout into the abyss and hope someone hears us. It's about making a concerted effort to educate the American people about what a regulated cannabis market can look like, and alter the dialogue about what it means to be a cannabis consumer. We have to hone our message, share it from the most reliable sources possible, and hope to change the course of history. The longer cannabis is forced to live in the shadows, the longer we inhibit the public from being able to make informed decisions about their own health.

INTERVIEW WITH DINA BROWNER

"Dr." Dina Browner is not a board-certified MD, nor did she go to medical school. She is, however, always quick to remind people of these facts. Known as "The Real Nancy Botwin," she's amassed a huge social media following, operates a nonprofit that helps victims of the war on drugs, and co-owns AHHS WeHo, named one of the best dispensaries in Los Angeles. She has consulted for TV shows like Disjointed *and* Sons of Anarchy; *she's been called the "queen of medical marijuana" by* Rolling Stone *and "Pot Doc to the Stars" by* Billboard *and* Variety. *To say Dina is a cannabis celebrity would be doing her a disservice, as she's so much more than that. We met while raising money for her charity, and it was clear that she wore many hats in the industry. I wanted to hear from someone who's been on the forefront of cannabis in California since its infancy.*

How'd you get the nickname Dr. Dina?

I was given the nickname Dr. Dina from the one and only Snoop Dogg. I didn't go to medical school, but I opened the first Medical Cannabis Doctor's office in Southern California in 2002. I helped Snoop acquire his first letter of recommendation from a licensed physician making him a legal medical cannabis patient. He immediately renamed me and would only refer to me as Dr. Dina from that day forward and has remained a patient of mine ever since. I originally met Snoop when I was fifteen years old. My friend's father was his criminal attorney. So this year makes twenty-nine years that we have been friends.

People say you're the real life Nancy Botwin. Can you talk to me about that?

It's a bit of a touchy subject for me. I wasn't consulted, paid, or asked to have a show based on me. I first heard about the show when a patient of mine walked into my dispensary and congratulated me on my new show. I had no clue as to what they were talking about. After asking some questions I realized there was a new billboard down the street that said *Weeds* on it. I was freaking out, since this was the early 2000s and being in the spotlight for cannabis could bring unwanted DEA attention. I thought it was a prank, and I called Snoop Dogg to yell at him for buying a billboard for me. When he had no idea what I was talking about, I realized that this wasn't a joke, and it was a real TV show. Once the show came out, I wrote down all the names in the credits at the end and searched them in my dispensary database. There they were, all patients of mine. Patients that spent a lot of time in the store asking questions that I naïvely answered. There are so many striking similarities between myself and the Nancy Botwin character, but there are many parts to the character that are not similar. I don't sleep with every person I meet, I don't kill grandmothers, and I don't sell cannabis to kids (unless that child is a medical patient and has their parents' permission). Also, I don't drink iced coffee, but I do always have a hot green tea in my hand. Although the character wasn't exactly like me, the show gave me a voice in the community.

I did open one of the first dispensaries in Southern California in 2003 and many of my staff members are represented in the show as characters. My right-hand man, Byrd, is the inspiration for Conrad and my old partner Andrew (who inspired Andy) is currently in jail for being an idiot, just like in the show.

You're one half of Freedom Grow. How did that start and what have you accomplished?

Freedom Grow was started out of love and necessity. I first met my partner Stephanie Landa when she walked into my dispensary to sell me cannabis in 2002. Soon after she began providing me with most of the cannabis products I sold at my shop. She ended up moving to San Francisco to a larger grow space and was busted by the police. They turned her case over to the DEA and she ended up serving five years in federal prison for growing medical cannabis. When Stephanie got out, she informed me of all the atrocities in prison and how badly prisoners rely on having commissary funds. Together we created FreedomGrow. org a 501(c)3 that raises funds to put on the books of nonviolent cannabis prisoners. We also help with clemency efforts, holiday drives for the prisoners and their children who suffer along with their incarcerated parent. We started off with a grassroots effort. We sell hot chocolate and slushees at cannabis events with all the funds going directly to the prisoners, since neither one of us takes a salary. Thanks to wonderful companies like Organa Brands, we have been able to help so many people. Our dream is for all cannabis prisoners to be given clemency and sent home to be with their families.

You're incredibly popular on social media. How has that impacted your business, and would your success have been possible without a large social media following?

This makes me laugh. When I first started my Instagram page, I had no clue it would become so popular. I was afraid to post anything cannabis related and I thought Instagram was a place where people posted pictures of their meals. It wasn't until I posted a picture of me with some of my celebrity friends did my page take off. Now, years later, it has become a huge platform for advertising what I do. It's amazing that I can reach out to anyone I want and they respond to me. I've made so many connections through social media. Instagram didn't build my business, but it helped! Also, being the first dispensary in Los Angeles County to be licensed to sell adult-use cannabis in 2018 didn't hurt either!

What brought you into this line of work?

I used to be in the fashion industry and I was able to make people feel good on the outside by dressing them in something that made them feel empowered. Now I make people feel good from the inside, which is way more meaningful to me.

I first got into the industry after a friend of mine was diagnosed with stage-four cancer. He wanted to give up. In fact, one day in 2001 he called me up and asked me to help him find a gun to end his life. He was so sick from the chemo, he was throwing up all of his pills. He had lost his medical insurance and was paying out of pocket for his treatments, and he couldn't hold his meds down. He decided he would kill himself and leave what was left in his bank account to his wife so she could bury him and start her life over. This wasn't an acceptable option for me. I immediately drove to his house with a joint. I forced him to smoke it with me, and after a few minutes of arguing with him, he conceded. He took three puffs and immediately stopped dry heaving. Color returned to his face and his stomach started to growl. He hadn't been able to eat or keep any food down. That night, he ate his first meal in almost two weeks, took his pills, and kept them down. "It's a miracle," he said. That moment changed the course of my history. I spent weeks looking for a doctor or dispensary to help him but there were none in Southern California. I finally found a doctor in San Francisco. I drove him to Northern California to acquire a doctor's recommendation for cannabis, and ended up partnering with his doctor and opening a clinic in West Hollywood a week later. Three months after that, I opened my first dispensary. I have been able to help so many people find safe access to cannabis in the seventeen years since. My friend was able to tolerate his treatment and has been in remission for fifteen years.

How has the industry changed since you started?

The industry I joined was definitely much different from the legal market I exist in now. There weren't many rules. We had to navigate on our own. Luckily for me, I was always surrounded by wonderful people who truly cared about the patients. I quickly learned what the word compassion meant. It wasn't just caring about someone. It was providing free medicine to people who truly needed it to survive. I remember joking with my partner, "Wouldn't it be nice if you could walk into Neiman Marcus and point to a pair of shoes you want and say 'I need compassion.'" That's how it worked in California pre-legalization. These days, we can't do that. The state needs its tax money. We prepay our distribution taxes before products are even sold. I used to make the rules for my business, now the state makes the rules and there are *so many of them*! I feel like we went from attending a fun, kids' summer camp to attending an intense Ivy League college overnight, without much preparation. 2018 was a year of learning, and I'm excited to see what 2019 brings.

Talking about the West Coast specifically. Give me broad strokes on your impression of the industry? Are things better now than they were? Can you remember a time when you couldn't find weed if you wanted it?

Although we have many hoops to jump through, the most important part of legalization to me is acceptance. Ever since I started my journey in the cannabis industry, I felt like I was looked down upon. My own father used to ask me the same question once a week for sixteen years: "When are you going to get out of this crazy industry and get yourself a real job?" Now he tells me how proud he is of me and is truly excited about all the projects I'm working on. That alone is worth it to me. I went from being "She's a drug dealer" to "She's a successful entrepreneur." I've also noticed the different types of people who walk into the shop, many of these people were afraid to be on a list and afraid to get a medical cannabis recommendation but now that it's legal they are open to trying cannabis for the first time. It's helping so many people.

Luckily, California is a cannabis mecca. I knew that when I first opened the shop, and had the attitude, "If you build it, they will come." We are known for our wonderful farmers, and I have never had any issues finding products for the shop. The major difference today is we can order products off a menu, and it gets delivered to us by a distribution company with an invoice, all individually packaged, lab-tested, branded, and taxed. Gone are the days of having one-pound turkey bags filled with cannabis dropped off at the shop. I don't miss packaging up and labeling products one bit. The one thing I do miss is the older strains that don't produce a high yield. Most licensed growers focus on high-yielding strains, so they don't bother with the smaller craft cannabis grows. OG Kush was one of the strains that was available everywhere until legalization hit. Now it's more difficult to find.

What's your best cannabis-related moment during your career?

I have had so many incredible moments that would never have happened if I wasn't in the industry. Having a patient tell you that they beat cancer because of me is the best feeling in the world. It's also a pretty amazing feeling to be star-struck over a famous customer, and have them be star-struck by meeting me. My best moment was when I got the news that a little one-year-old boy named Waldo, that I was treating for bilateral retinoblastoma, was in remission and the surgeon didn't have to remove his eyes as they previously thought. "It's a miracle" is always what the doctors say, but I know it was the cannabis that helped him. His parents found me online, so if I never entered the industry, would Waldo have lost his vision? This is what keeps me going to work every day.

Tell me about consulting for television shows? How did it happen, and what's been the best part of adding that to your list of accomplishments?

Consulting for TV shows is so much fun. I get to be surrounded by amazing and talented people on the top of their game. I have sat in many writers' rooms and explained how the industry works. As soon as I arrive on set, everyone has questions for me, usually personal. Cast, crew, legal—everyone has questions about cannabis—and they trust me to walk them through the process of finding what would work for them. My proudest moment in consulting was while I was working on *Disjointed*. I was able to convince the executive producers, Chuck Lorre and David Javerbaum, that we needed to spotlight some important themes. One was the story line about Carter, the security guard, and how he was dealing with PTSD from serving in Iraq. Another major story line was when the shop was raided by the DEA for no apparent reason. I wanted to show the public that we suffered at the hands of the government even when we were doing everything correctly according to the state medical cannabis laws. I think it was the very first time this was ever shown on TV.

Any other stories from _Disjointed_?

I spent every weekday for a year on set with Kathy Bates. She is by far the most talented woman I've ever met. The first day on set everyone was nervous about meeting her. We all feared her Annie Wilkes character from _Misery_ and she played it up. She walked onto the set wearing a glamorous, feather-trimmed shawl, looked around the room with a very serious look, like she was about to pull out a sledgehammer and start beating us all. Then she loudly announced, "I'm ready for you motherfuckers. Where is the weed? Let's do this!" She quickly became one of my favorite people on the planet. Kathy is a breast cancer survivor and she is the face of the lymphedema society. She is a very special lady.

Imagine you're a kid again. I tell you that one day you're going to be _the_ name that many people associated with weed. What's your reaction as a kid? What is it now?

Teenage Dina would say, "No way, Jose. I'm a good girl!" That said, I still find it strange that people associate my name with cannabis, since cannabis is so much bigger than me. It's been around forever, but I am totally cool with the fact that I might have made it a little less scary or intimidating for people.

Talk to me about sales in terms of flower. What's the trend there and where do you see it going?

Flowers, to me, are raw goods, or working material, although I occasionally enjoy smoking a joint. I prefer hash oil so the flowers need to be processed first. Flowers used to be 80 percent of my business with edibles at 15 percent and vape pens 5 percent. Now I would say that flowers make up 40 percent, vapes 30 percent, edibles 20 percent, and topicals 10 percent. Clearly the vape market is becoming huge. People don't want to smoke but they are open to vaping. It's discrete, and you don't smell like you just smoked a joint.

Can you talk to me about potency and how that plays into sales within your dispensaries?

When we operated as a medical cannabis dispensary prior to legalization, we could sell products that were very potent. One of our most popular edibles was a 1,000 mg chocolate bar. Patients would buy it and cut it up into several pieces and it would last them a good while. Now that it's become legalized, we are limited to selling edibles at 100 mg total. This was a big change for people. They now have to spend more money to get the dosage they need. On a positive note, we haven't had the headlines that Colorado first had when they legalized with people reporting they had eaten too much cannabis.

CHAPTER 12

Darkness

Disruption has never been a stranger to me. The moment it seems things are settling into place and there is some semblance of stability on the road ahead, things change. Perhaps it is just the natural ebb and flow of life for some, but for others, there is an underlying addiction to chaos—to the freshness of starting everything over again. I have always related to the latter group. And why not? There's something fascinating about living several lives in the same lifetime. I've gone from straight-A prep school kid to a straight-C college student, from drug addiction to sober living, from a certifiable bachelor to a partner in a committed and loving relationship. If what we fear most in life is the unknown, why not embrace it? Hell, screw embracing it. Why not make it a part of our DNA? Embracing chaos, rather than working diligently to avoid it, became impossibly intertwined with my own existence. It dawned on me that perhaps I'd been using all of my expendable energy to stifle something that was, at its core, a part of me. I'm not saying that a life of chaos—moving once a year over the course of a decade, making major life decisions on a whim, or moving in with your boyfriend after three months—is for everyone. What I am suggesting is a life of *managed* chaos. To live with some sense of freedom, we must embrace the inherent uncertainty of what it means to be a human being.

"What do you think about moving to Saint Thomas?"

My boss had telephoned to pitch the idea. It didn't sound so bad, truth be told. Los Angeles is a great place to live, but a horrible place to drive. As someone who spends more time in a car than in a bed, the thought of posting up on a nice little island in the middle of nowhere sounded like a revelation. A week earlier, as a joke, Michael and I had attended the inauguration of Donald Trump. A certain gay politician had gifted us tickets. We all agreed it would be a funny jab to have a handsome gay couple sitting up front. We made our way to Washington, D.C., and checked into a W Hotel near the site of the event. It was the first moment it became clear to me the extent to which I really had been living in a bubble, insulated against the rage that had been simmering in so much of this country. The fate of cannabis, as a result of the political regime change, was now hanging in the balance. We walked into the inauguration, took one look at the crowd, and promptly departed. For some reason, the idea of spending a morning with Mike Pence just didn't seem like a great use of time. Instead, we had brunch and marched in a protest through the capital streets in true homosexual fashion. We went to a farewell dinner with some friends, gagged on a horrible dish known as a "liquified olive" at what was supposed to be a chic restaurant, and promptly boarded a plane to the US Virgin Islands.

Arriving in Saint Thomas felt like a scene from *The Thomas Crown Affair* (the Pierce Brosnan version, of course), thanks in no small part to the calypso music I'd been blaring through my headphones during the entire flight. We headed to the rental car stand, and it was like nothing I'd ever seen before. Though branded with the name of a major car rental company, the bumper was hanging off the front of the car they delivered to us. There were dents covering every visible inch, and the instrument panel lit up like a firework upon ignition. This, I suppose, was the fate of an island car when mainlanders were entrusted to successfully embrace the absurd task of driving on the left-hand side of the road. Two of the owners of our company were already living in Saint Thomas, at the farthest point of the island from the airport, in a gorgeous beachfront home. We arrived in the early hours of the morning and went straight to sleep. There were no curtains in the room, so we were awoken promptly at six thanks to a combination of the rising sun, the meowing of stray cats, and the screaming of roosters, which sounded as if they knew they were on their way to a Chick-fil-A processing plant. There are countless incentives for businesses to relocate to the Caribbean, as few mainland companies are willing to bolster the local economies of remote island towns. The perks range from more favorable personal income tax rates, to the less quantifiable knowledge that you're bringing jobs to an area that's been plagued by a defunct economy for most of its modern existence. Ever the dreamers, a few people from the leadership team thought we might explore the feasibility of having a remote office, and thus, Michael and I found ourselves on a yet another company workation in the middle of nowhere.

We spent the next ten days exploring the island, working on our tans, and taking in the scenery. It was a beautiful place, but something seemed odd about it. We chartered a boat one afternoon, and the captain informed Michael and me that we were the first gay couple he'd ever met. I laughed as he told me, but he met my eyes and looked away. *Holy shit, this guy is serious!* As it turns out, Saint Thomas is not ranked among the most friendly locales toward those identifying as LGBTQ. It had quickly become apparent that living in Saint Thomas might not be ideal.

We returned to Los Angeles and I settled back into work. Adult-use cannabis was legal across the state, and dispensaries were beginning to pop up like weeds. Working remotely, I'd had the luxury over the past two years to take 90 percent of my conference calls in bed, and with Michael now working for the same company, having a companion there with me was a welcome respite from the years of solitude. Most people thought we were crazy for dating and working together, but it worked for us. It's been many years since we first met, and I'm happy to report we still love spending every waking moment together, much to the chagrin of my friends and Instagram followers.

In the middle of 2017, I received another call about relocating. Jeremy was on the other line, curious to know if we'd ever consider moving to Puerto Rico. We booked a few tickets, and a group from the main office flew out to spend a week getting to know the island. It was beautiful, warm, and not unlike Los Angeles in terms of soul-crushing traffic. Cannabis was just becoming legal in Puerto Rico, so it had been decided we would set up an office in San Juan. We returned to Los Angeles, packed up our things, and prepared to leave our old life behind. Once again, just as things seemed to be settling, we were out the door and off to the next adventure. The patchwork of cannabis laws often requires that business owners relocate to new and emerging markets in order to stay competitive. There is, inherent in the industry, a first-mover advantage. The thought is, the first team to set up shop and begin gobbling up resources will be the business which ultimately reigns supreme. And, perhaps, the patchwork of the human psyche requires the same in order to keep one's edge. Or maybe I'm just impulsive—who can say?

About two weeks before we were set to depart for San Juan, Hurricane Irma headed toward the Caribbean. Some from our company were already living in Puerto Rico, and braced themselves for the storm. I studied the news daily in an effort to make some sense of not only what was to come, but what would happen in the aftermath. By some small miracle, the hurricane largely missed San Juan, and aside from downed power lines and issues with other utilities, the island was spared. We all counted our blessings and assumed the worst was behind us. Oh, how wrong we were.

Within ten days, a tropical depression was brewing some 1,000 miles from San Juan, and with each passing day the storm grew more intense as it edged toward the island. Because Irma had proven to not live up to the hype, many people, including our friends and colleagues, remained on the island as the storm approached despite the warnings to leave, the so-called Irma effect. The resulting storm was one of the worst in history, leaving nearly 3,000 dead. We struggled to make sense of what had become of our new home, as lack of internet and power made it nearly impossible to communicate with those on the ground. Desperate to get our friends to safety, we attempted to get a prop plane to fly from the Dominican Republic to rural San Juan in a pseudo-evacuation attempt. Without a functioning FAA, the plane had no ability to land due to a lack of air-traffic control operations. Our friends were some of the lucky ones, and just made one of the last commercial flights out of San Juan in the days following Maria.

I eventually connected with a mutual friend through the celebrity gifting department and was put in touch with a particularly charitable celebrity, whom I worked with to source private jets used to bring supplies to Puerto Rico. In the two months following the hurricane, our team was able to bring more than thirty million pounds of supplies into the storm-ravaged island. Organa Brands made a sizable donation to help fund the efforts, as we had already developed a strong love for our new home. Ten days after the hurricane and after already giving up our apartment in LA, Michael and I boarded a plane and set course for San Juan. Approaching the island was like a scene from some post-apocalyptic film. Blue FEMA tarps covered every roof for as far as the eye could see, trees were bent and twisted, and broken glass covered the streets like confetti after a parade. We slowly regained access to utilities and standard services, and began to settle into our new home. There was, of course, still work to be done.

Puerto Rico, like many medical marijuana markets, offers patients a perplexing assortment of laws. Originally banned in 1932, cannabis was legalized for medical use in 2015. Though it took close to two years for the program to get up and running, by 2017 there were more than 34,000 patients registered in the system. By February 2019, there were over 59,000 patients and seventy-one active cannabis dispensaries, far outpacing many mainland states, such as Massachusetts, which has 59,000 registered patients served by just fourteen dispensaries. The rapid expansion on a remote island is nothing short of a miracle. It's important to understand that Puerto Rico, as a territory, is largely conservative. A poll conducted in 2013 found that 70 percent of Puerto Ricans were opposed to legalization. It wasn't until 2015 when an executive order from Governor Alejandro García Padilla that Puerto Rico would enter the wild world of legalized cannabis. García Padilla believed his nation was "taking a significant step in the area of health that is fundamental to our development and quality of life," showing his belief that legal cannabis is not just beneficial to patients, but to the economy, as well. This green wave didn't come without restrictions, though. Laws in the territory ban the smoking of marijuana, thus it can only be ingested or used in a vaporizer.

For all its beauty, living in San Juan was like stepping back in time. Coming from the cannabis-soaked bastion of free-will that is Los Angeles, I was met with a strange mix of both hope and sadness to see cannabis struggling to emerge as a mainstream good. For a US territory plagued by a financial crisis, it's difficult to find ways in which a regulated market wouldn't help restore some of the island's grandeur. Beyond that, if Puerto Rico is one day able to offer adult-use cannabis, it would surely become the spring break capital of the Caribbean. Who isn't interested in sunny beaches, great food, and easy access to weed? Colorado and California experienced massive growth in just my own short time working in the industry, and business was still on the rise. In our shared office space, a particular front-desk worker had popped her head in to see if anyone was interested in purchasing a few vape cartridges. Curious, I asked the price. My jaw fell on the floor as she explained that they were available in packs of four and cost nearly $400. As someone who makes a living from well-regulated cannabis sales, I saw it as both a tragedy for the people of Puerto Rico, who deserve reasonable and safe access to cannabis, and a chilling example of what happens to the bottom line before legalization can take hold. We've already established that a person who doesn't support a regulated market, by default supports a black market. Such was the case here, as skyrocketing prices for legal cannabis purchases were certainly driving more business to the illegal drug trade. When cannabis is legalized, consumers are able to support regulated enterprises that offer safe products at reasonable prices. When it remains either fully illegal or only pseudo-legal, well, we had the evidence of the results right in front of us. That's not to say that regulation inherently lowers all prices across the board. In many instances, prices can go up. In places like Washington State, for example, the taxes are so high that only a small percentage of people have transitioned away from buying black-market cannabis to purchasing within the confines of the law. The overarching result of regulation, however, is that once there is a legal framework to operate within, more and more businesses open their doors, and the resulting competition generally drives the actual cost of goods to a much lower point.

And what about the human cost of a black market? All across the United States, people sit in prison cells facing a range of sentences for nonviolent cannabis possession. Some, depending on the state in which they were charged, may face life sentences. Others, in places like Denver, can be given a citation and pay a small fine for the same or similar offenses. This disparity in sentencing is, at its core, one of the most troubling aspects of the patchwork cannabis laws across the country. According to the Drug Policy Alliance, an industry watchdog, the US government spends nearly $50 billion each year fighting the so-called War on Drugs. In 2017 alone, half a million Americans were arrested and charged for simple cannabis possession, despite the thirty-three states with some form of legalization.

Across the country, 200,000 students have lost federal student loans or financial aid over drug charges, contributing to a vicious cycle of financial instability. More horrifying still are the men and women serving *life sentences* for nonviolent drug crimes. Some of these prisoners, such as Alice Marie Johnson, have gained national attention. After twenty-one years, Johnson had her life sentence commuted in 2018, with the help of Kim Kardashian. A recent *Washington Post* article, citing the Sentencing Project, found 1,907 federal prisoners are currently serving life sentences for drug charges. At $32,000 per prisoner per year, the federal government spends some $64 million each year housing these prisoners. And that's just federal prison. At the state level, more than 200,000 Americans are serving life sentences for the same types of nonviolent crimes. It's also important to factor into the cost that these are people who could otherwise be working, paying taxes, and contributing to the economic health of the country. According to The Sentencing Project:

> *A series of law enforcement and sentencing policy changes of the "tough on crime" era resulted in dramatic growth in incarceration. Since the official beginning of the War on Drugs in 1982, the number of people incarcerated for drug offenses in the US skyrocketed from 40,900 in 1980 to 450,345 in 2016. Today, there are more people behind bars for a drug offense than the number of people who were in prison or jail for any crime in 1980.*

From corrupt prison administrations to subhuman living conditions to a lack of access to proper medical care, a life sentence is seemingly designed to be nearly unbearable. And while I agree there are many crimes worthy of such a sentence, to my mind drug violations fail to meet the standard for what should constitute such a punishment. Enter Freedom Grow. Founded by Stephanie Landa and Dr. Dina, the real-life Nancy Botwin, this nonprofit seeks to make a change in the lives of those serving life sentences for nonviolent cannabis charges. There are few options when it comes to making a prison sentence more humane, but the most immediate impact is felt in the prison commissary account. For those lucky enough to have financial support from friends and family on the outside, these accounts allow these prisoners—or Pot POWs as they're known at Freedom Grow—to buy basic necessities like toothbrushes, snacks, soap, and paper. Small things many of us take for granted make all the difference for those on the inside. I first met Stephanie and Dr. Dina in the lead-up to our annual charity golf tournament. The pair had met some years earlier after shared experiences in the cannabis world. Stephanie had been arrested for cannabis cultivation in 2002 despite it being legal at the state level in California, and quickly realized that a commissary account was the difference between misery and some semblance of dignity while serving time. After being released, she started Freedom Grow, and began selling hot chocolate at various cannabis-centric events. They would take the resulting money, use it to purchase money orders, and fund accounts inside prison walls. After hunting high and low for the perfect philanthropic partner, I was introduced to Freedom Grow and found that they shared in our beliefs that until we can free all nonviolent drug offenders, we should be striving to remind them that they are not forgotten. It seems unfair, cruel even, to think that while many cannabis businesses thrive in a regulated market, there are all those people behind bars who have been forgotten in the wake of the green rush. The charity's mission is simple—to provide a lifeline to the outside world for those incarcerated. Through financial contributions, Freedom Grow is able to add money to the commissary accounts of those whose families lack the financial resources to do so, or for those who simply have been forgotten by the outside world.

Upon meeting, it was instantly clear that not only was Freedom Grow's mission one that any reasonable person could support, but was being led by two people who had devoted their lives to healing the damage done by the drug war. Clemency is a dream often out of reach for many of those behind bars, for the simple fact that they are not in a financial position to fight for it. In order to apply for clemency, those serving these sentences must fill out hundreds of pages of legal documents, often without the help of an attorney. The only instrument available for most of them to draft the necessary documents is a typewriter. A recent *New Yorker* article profiled the high costs, nearly equal to the price of a laptop, associated with the typed word from inside America's prison. Ink spools cost eight dollars a piece, and prisoners can expect to burn through close to a dozen before completing a clemency filing. In order to apply to see the outside world once again, there's a higher cost than just the 300-odd dollars associated with purchasing a typewriter. The real cost is a continued lack of freedom. If you're lucky enough to find yourself employed while in prison, wages pile up at mere pennies per hour, making a bearable—or better yet, free—life simply out of reach. With the help of organizations like Freedom Grow, there is a glimmer of hope for those impacted by the war on drugs.

Of course, the vast number of people serving time for nonviolent drug charges is merely a symptom of a much larger issue—the War on Drugs and the ways in which it disproportionately impacts people of color. In the United States, African Americans account for 74 percent of those imprisoned for drug possession, according to a recent position paper by the ACLU. The racially charged roots of the War on Drugs date back to the 1900s, when images of people of color were used to stoke fears about the impact of drugs in the country, resulting in a century-long battle to unwind the racism that is inextricably connected with the perception of drugs in America. We need not look any further than Jimmy Buffett's "Pencil Thin Mustache," where he sings that "only jazz musicians were smokin' marijuana," to understand how the socio-political climate surrounding cannabis painted it as dangerous drug. Released in 1974, the song was written as a nod to the culture of the 1950s, a time when reefer madness still had a stronghold on a nation. It's impossible to discuss the War on Drugs without talking about the racial disparity inherent in criminal cannabis charges. On average, a person of color is almost four times more likely to be charged with cannabis possession than a white person. In lieu of the commonly used term cannabis, Harry Anslinger, who ran the Federal Bureau of Narcotics from 1930 through the mid-1960s, popularized the word marijuana. His use of that particular spelling was rooted in deep anti-immigrant sentiments due in large part to the legal immigration of close to one million Mexican citizens into the United States. The goal was to make the drug appear foreign, and thus linked with the racially charged rhetoric of the time. One of the more horrifying quotes attributed to Anslinger is:

> *"How many murders, suicides, robberies, criminal assaults, holdups, burglaries and deeds of maniacal insanity it causes each year, especially among the young, can only be conjectured.... No one knows, when he places a marijuana cigarette to his lips, whether he will become a joyous reveler in a musical heaven, a mad insensate, a calm philosopher, or a murderer..."*

Jesus Christ, what a tool. One of Anslinger's allies, William Randolph Hearst, was more than happy to amplify the so-called "race connection" between cannabis and immigrants, and so began the early stages of the War on Drugs.

It wasn't until Ronald Reagan took office that the country's drug policy saw its most treacherous leap forward, with the advent of mandatory sentencing laws. According to The Drug Policy Alliance, the number of individuals incarcerated for drug violations increased from 50,000 in 1980 to more than 400,000 by 1997, due largely to a staggering departure from the drug policies of years past. In 2018, we still feel the massive repercussions from a century of failed drug policies. The modern reincarnations of Nancy Reagan who shout "just say no" from the rooftop of the nearest dispensary, soon find themselves investing in a local grower. Drugs are bad.

Cannabis is immoral. Stoners should all get a real jobs. The great hypocrisy here is that cannabis is only wrong until those in power say otherwise. The disruptors of the cannabis industry aren't just working to create a new stream of income within the US economy, but to unwind failed drug policy, free wrongly convicted prisoners, and pay dues to those who suffered as a result of a now-booming and pseudo-legal industry.

INTERVIEW WITH TRACIE EGAN MORRISSEY

Tracie Egan Morrissey is an award-winning development executive who has led teams at Viceland and Broadly, and was the founding editor at Jezebel. She covers topics like politics, women's rights, fashion, and cannabis. We first met in the early days of our VIP Gifting program, and now bond over Real Housewives. I was interested to hear the perception of cannabis from someone living on the East Coast, and how that compares to those we've heard from living in legal states.

How has the perception of cannabis changed over the years, specifically in the media?

It's definitely become much more accepted. I think that's probably because more stoners are in positions of making and green-lighting content, resulting in a landscape that's not as square.

You started *Jezebel* and then went on to Vice. How did these two outlets cover cannabis in ways that were different from other outlets?

The biggest difference is that these outlets don't treat cannabis as a drug or a taboo thing. The POV is that smoking a joint is akin to drinking a glass of wine—but maybe not as harmful. Specifically, Vice had a digital show called *Weediquette* that later evolved into a longform series for its basic cable network Viceland. The show focused on the burgeoning "green" economy, its impact on society, and the different uses of cannabis—including those outside of recreation, like treating PTSD and children with cancer.

Do you think your work has lessened the stigma around cannabis? In what ways?

I really hope so! I think I've helped, in my own small way, to change people's perception of moms who smoke pot. It's possible to be a good, doting parent and provider and also enjoy marijuana in your free time.

Are you seeing people in your social circles becoming less shy about cannabis? What's that attributed to?

Yes I have. I think it's a general cultural shift, but like with most cultural shifts in America, a lot of this can be attributed to marketing. With the legalization of marijuana, companies are free to market their products in a specific way that speaks to people who would've normally felt like cannabis use was for "hippies" or "stoners." Now there are companies that are telling women that their products can help them orgasm or manage their menstrual cramps.

Where do you see the future heading for cannabis in the United States?

I think that in the direction we're headed as a country, access to cannabis will be more safe and legal than women's access to essential health care.

Cannabis is often a punchline for many media outlets, but that's not been the case at Vice. Was there a concerted effort to elevate the conversation around cannabis?

That was definitely a goal with the evolving cannabis coverage at Vice. However, now that the rest of the country is coming around to the benign nature of marijuana and legalizing it for recreation, I think the coverage can switch back to being more fun and less babies-with-cancer.

How long before we see a weed ad run during the Super Bowl?

I think we're probably a ways off from seeing a weed ad during the Super Bowl. There's too much hypocrisy and lack of logic in that organization about what is socially acceptable. They can have multiple accused rapists and wife beaters on the field at one time, but they fine and bench players who test positive for marijuana. Janet Jackson was fined and banned for partially showing one nipple, but we were subjected to *both* of Adam Levine's during Maroon 5's halftime show. I don't expect the NFL or any of its affiliates to be socially progressive.

Going to NYU in the late '90s, how did cannabis culture of that era differ from the present?

I think, at the time, all we really had in terms of cannabis culture was *Half Baked* and *Dazed and Confused*. And maybe Phish concerts. At the time, I would've never smoked pot openly on the street for fear of getting arrested. But now, it just seems really normalized. The streets smell a whole lot better anyway.

CHAPTER 13

The Big, Bad,
(Revenue-Generating) Wolf

Cannabis is changing. There's no denying it. The marijuana of my parent's generation is nothing more than a faint memory when compared to the potency of both product and branding of today's cannabis. Indeed, the industry has recruited the best and brightest to help move its product, and make them both appealing and safe. A regulated market makes pot dealers obsolete—why buy a dimebag from your local bartender in the parking lot out back when you can walk into a dispensary and be treated to a shopping experience more akin to Fred Segal than 7-Eleven? Of course, this new retail frontier didn't appear out of thin air. It's been carefully curated and manufactured from the ground up by teams of marketing gurus, PR professionals, and digital-media experts. Labs create products using the best R&D teams available, while the marketing teams design packaging and execute advertising campaigns. And it's not just the packaging that's changed, but the actual consumable products. There's been an increased demand for new and dynamic product offerings, and consequently, more people than ever are visiting dispensaries for the first time. We're seeing people who have never tried weed buy cannabis-infused chocolate bars, or infused bubble bath, or even cannabis beers, all intoxicants sold alongside the more traditional flower products. The regulated market has created a path for novice cannabis consumers to dip their toes into the pool without the experience subjecting them to the back-alley transactions and subsequent low-quality products of previous generations. Look no further than Sunset Boulevard to see millions of dollars at work, selling cannabis products from every vertical across any number of gleaming dispensaries dotting the urban sprawl. Stoners of generations past may call them *big cannabis sellouts*, while others laud them for making products safer and more accessible.

For obvious reasons, I align with the latter. Big cannabis isn't really that big...not yet, at least. The industry is still in its infancy, and businesses like ours are setting up the framework for what a federally legal arena will look like in its final form. From packaging, to R&D, to sales and marketing, cannabis is, in many ways, just like any other fast-moving consumer goods company. We make products, we package them, we wholesale them to retailers, and the consumer purchases them from behind the counter. It's a process we, as consumers, are all familiar with. So why, then, is cannabis still so scary to so many?

Altering perceptions is a long game, and while there have been enormous strides made in the last five years to truly bring cannabis into the forefront of American life, there is still a great deal of work to be done. Peter Davis, former editor of *Paper Magazine* and man-about-town in New York, told me, "Before legalization started to happen, cannabis was taboo and seen as a dangerous drug. Now, people cite the healing properties of cannabis and don't see it as a drug in the same way they do cocaine, or other illegal substances. It's definitely a new age for cannabis."

As I write this, Colorado has just celebrated its five-year anniversary of legalized recreational marijuana. Throughout that time, there was a lot of speculation among more mainstream conservative press as to the reliability of the results the communities in the state were seeing. Sure, this is great, but can it last? Many argued that the novel aspect of cannabis would wear off, people would lose interest, and the industry would return to its prior standing as something people only discussed in private. Five years in, and I'm here to say that, yeah, the business is here to stay. In year one, the state saw some $67 million in tax revenue; in 2018, we saw that number jump to $260 million. The result has been $927 million of tax proceeds generated directly from cannabis sales over the last five years. The state of Colorado charges 17.9 percent sales tax on cannabis products, in addition to whatever local taxes apply. The rate of drug arrests have decreased, though African Americans are still twice as likely to receive criminal charges relating to drugs—for all the progress that has been made on the economic front, the social arena leaves much to be desired. The reality is that federal legalization may still be years away.

The great question, of course, is how does such a beloved substance continue to face countless legal challenges at every turn? According to a 2018 study from the Pew Research Center, 61 percent of Americans now support the legalization of cannabis, almost doubling since 2001. The study also found that there are large generational differences in support, with an obvious majority among Gen X, Millennials, and a handful of Baby Boomers. Only 39 percent of The (not so) Silent generation support such federal changes, which perhaps explains the roadblocks faced by cannabis supporters. With 74 percent of the 2017–2018 Congress having been born between 1928 and 1964, there appears to be some correlation between the political change brought about by our elected officials and their generation's misaligned views with regards to the youth in America. My theory is that as the current political regime ages out of power, replaced by increasingly young and diverse Americans, we will see a dramatic shift in our country's drug policy. Only time will tell, of course. If not for my stint in rehab and some less-than-savory Facebook photos, I might consider running for political office myself.

The real fight, when it comes to cannabis, is less about the actual plant, and more about the ideas it represents. We've already discussed the ways in which cannabis is linked to racial inequality throughout American history, but the second piece of that puzzle lies in human perception. The notion of the stoner spending all day in the basement playing *Fortnite* and masturbating to anime porn is one I've gone to great lengths to combat. While I'm sure there are many cannabis users who do just that, they are the minority. I would, however, like to introduce a new concept, the idea of the *new silent majority*, those who use cannabis in the privacy of their own homes, with their trusted friends, and without any intention of discussing it in wide social circles. The reality is many Americans smoke weed, roughly one in seven according to a 2017 poll from *Reuters*. It is the ardent supporters of the cause who make news headlines and demonstrate in parks on 4/20, but it is the average moms and dads and professionals who have found cannabis to be an integral part of their weekly or sometimes daily ritual. Much in the same way that I slather La Mer eye cream on three times a day or down shots of lemon and ginger, a new generation of cannabis users have found that it aids in their overall well-being. In places like Aspen, we've seen cannabis sales outpace those of alcohol, and I suspect this trend will continue. By 2022, conservative estimates place cannabis sales in the United States at $55 billion. When you compare those figures to the alcohol industry, a business with an estimated $73 billion in annual sales today, it's hard to deny the notion that cannabis will soon surpass alcohol in both value and availability. Behind the scenes, it is the person you'd never expect who props up a booming industry.

An image of a Phish sweatshirt covered in pizza stains and adorned with a wire-wrapped opal necklace is no longer the image that comes to mind when picturing the modern cannabis user, and the root cause lies in a slow erosion of the stereotypes that used to plague us. It simply takes one mom at her book club extolling the virtues of taking a quarter of an edible at night to help her sleep. Suddenly, the rest of the group is joining in on the fun. As human beings, we look to others to know how to act. Early in my life, I would have never contemplated the idea of being a cannabis user, because it did not align with my self-prescribed image. For the bulk of my youth, I spent Friday nights with my grandmother, watching Charlie Chan movies, cooking up booze-free Kahlúa, and living a quiet life shrouded from outside influence. It wasn't until my junior year of high school that I first started watching *Queer as Folk* in secret on my laptop. That was where I first recall seeing people smoking weed as part of a normal life. I eventually had to Google the term "roach clip" to find out why a few of the characters were holding what looked to be scissors up to their mouths when smoking. Come to find out, the goal was to get every last bit of weed out of the joint, a testament to both the cost and scarcity of cannabis during the era of the show's filming. It was in those first few exposures to the world of pot, that I first began to imagine myself as someone who might try it. Don't mistake me, I hardly blame the impact of the media on what would later develop into a full-blown addiction to all sorts of drugs, but seeing someone on a screen who was *like me* who also *smoked weed* made me feel oddly soothed. Maybe being perfect wasn't the goal any longer—maybe, the goal was just being happy.

Many years later, I set out to do just that—find some joy. It wasn't until I was sitting in a room filled with other addicts that I realized that most of us were looking for relief from mental anguish in the form of physical substances. It may sound crazy, but only around my third week of treatment did I began to see the ways in which addicts, myself included, use drugs to fill a void in their existence. There are countless people in the world who can use drugs recreationally and find that they have zero negative impact on their lives or livelihoods. For many of the people I've met in sobriety, drugs were never a value-add, they weren't a choice, nor were they an occasional thing. They were a requirement, a necessity, something as essential as water or air.

The experiences of an addict and those of a "normal" person have few, if any, similarities. Most who try an assortment of drugs don't devolve into smoking Percocet off of aluminum foil in a dark apartment, but that is the peril of addiction. Doing drugs does not, in fact, make someone cool. It doesn't make them more or less of anything, but is simply added to a list of recreational activities along with hiking, cooking, and screaming at the television during *Top Chef*. Of course, there are more negative analogs, like eating too many fried foods, or having a short fuse during an argument. The point I'm trying to convey here is that drug use is not a singularly defining characteristic for any human being.

The idea that cannabis is a gateway drug is a flawed one instilled in us by years of indoctrination from D.A.R.E. and similar anti-drug campaigns. From my own experience, addiction is a disease rooted deeply in our genetics, and either a person is born an addict or they are not. Certainly, environmental factors can play a role, but the notion that consuming cannabis as an adult will then lead to harder drugs is simply not rooted in fact or experience. And although no one is advocating for teenagers to use cannabis, Margaret Haney, director of the Marijuana Research Laboratory at Columbia University, was recently quoted in Vice saying, "I take umbrage when I see scientists saying there's a causal relationship between marijuana and negative brain outcomes."

What we really have on our hands is an issue that arrives twofold. One, as a misaligned sense of self; the other, in the form of societal pressure to align with existing social norms. Like any great social movement, the cannabis industry finds itself as the central disrupter in a long history of taboo subjects. In the last decade, and particularly in the last three years, cannabis has shifted from a tool of the counterculture, to a mainstay of household conversations. It wasn't until the layperson began to think, perhaps erroneously—"hey, maybe I could get rich off of this, legally!"—that we began to see a large shift in support for removing the stigma around not only consuming cannabis, but simply *discussing* it. And it's there, in those conversations at home, that the cannabis movement has gained its most powerful momentum. What was once the dog whistle for disparaging so-called lower companions, has now transformed into a booming industry powered largely by curiosity around a substance that remains so foreign to so many.

Not so long ago, my phone lit up with a FaceTime call from a distant relative. She was calling to say she was high as a kite and had never had so much fun. She was experiencing the effects of cannabis for the first time in thirty years, and she was over the moon.

"Jackson," she said. "This is a revelation. I haven't laughed this hard in years."

Not too long before that, I delivered some O.penVAPE pens to another relative who had undergone treatment for cancer. He could no longer drink, but sought some kind of intoxicant while playing the back nine at his country club. What was initially met with side-eye glares by members of his foursome soon became a weekly staple in which they were all partaking. It was all thanks to the simple fact that they could get a buzz while golfing, without fear of causing liver damage or needing to pee at the clubhouse every thirty minutes. This cultural shift has reverberated across ages, genders, and socio-economic statuses throughout the country, and is evidenced in large part by the shift in the media landscape surrounding the topic.

Look no further than television to see this dramatic shift in play. *Weeds*, perhaps the most popular series centered on cannabis, began airing in 2005, long before the recreational cannabis boom. The show portrays the illicit side of cannabis, focused on backroom dealmaking, suburban pot sales, and, of course, a heavy dose of murder. The crime aspect of the show drew viewers into what, at the time, was a largely realistic view of the flawed perceptions of cannabis in America. In 2018, we've seen cannabis emerge not as a central theme of a show (though there are plenty of those, too), but as a realistic depiction of the legal vices of the modern era. *Broad City*, on Comedy Central, portrays two young women living in the city, whose lives often involve the use of cannabis. They light up a joint before heading to a bougie dinner, and mix cannabis oil into a smoothie for post-op pain relief. Shows like Netflix's *Disjointed* offer a sometimes murky view of life behind the counter at a dispensary, though we do get a glimpse of the modern advocate and the ways in which cannabis activism can transform into a lucrative business. We see cannabis consumed in blockbuster films, and in shows like *Modern Family*—whereas ten years ago, a scene depicting consequence-free cannabis use in a primetime family sitcom would be not just unheard of, but scandalous. Shows like HBO's *Silicon Valley* depict frequent marijuana use, though just like the average consumer, the show's protagonist fails to destroy their life as a result. We've seen the dialogue around cannabis use shift across television and movies in the last five years. Most notably, cannabis seems to have been repositioned from nothing more than a punchline to a value-add in the lives of the people who consume it. Moreover, in shows like *High Maintenance*, the protagonist, a bicycle-riding pot dealer, pops in and out of the lives of his customers, adding dialogue to the diverse makeup of the modern consumer and the ways in which cannabis seamlessly integrates into their day-to-day lives.

It's not just in the media that cannabis and its derivatives have become popularized. Gracias Madre, a vegan staple of the LA restaurant scene, announced they'd be serving CBD cocktails as a regular part of their cocktail list. The Standard hotel in downtown Los Angeles opened a pop-up CBD dispensary in one of their outposts, and made headline news in doing so. Even back east, the James Hotel in New York conjured up a CBD-infused dinner menu, sparking joy in patrons looking not just for a good meal, but for something that offers the chance to *feel* better. CBD massages have become popular across the country, and customers are lining up for the chance to dip a toe into the weed pool. In 2018, CBD sales increased a whopping 1,700 percent, thanks in large part to increased media attention to the benefits of the compound.

I have several friends who, despite being sober members of AA, rely on topical cannabis products to aid in chronic pain and health issues. When presented with the choice, most of the people I know who suffer from debilitating illnesses choose cannabis products over opiates every time, despite the stigma that surrounds them in the larger landscape of sober communities. For many, their prior drugs of choice were indeed opiates, and before the expansion of the cannabis market, many recovering addicts were left with a horrific choice: suffer chronic pain or take a daily pill that may well lead them back down the road of addiction. One friend in particular found that the only possible relief from an excruciating spinal injury was a topical low-dose THC/CBD cream. It's been two years since that regimen started, and he lives a life absent the pain that had crippled him for years, all while staying sober and attending meetings—something that likely would not have been possible had he started on a prescription pain management program.

What do a TV show, an AA meeting, and a CBD cocktail have to do with one another? The three paint an important picture of the dramatic shift in cannabis over the last several years, all pointing to one central idea: the cannabis industry, and those working within it, have caused a disruption to the central beliefs of a vast swath of the American population. Old ideas about what it means to consume cannabis have been thrown out and replaced by the consensus that, used responsibly, cannabis can offer marked improvements in people's lives. Cannabis has shifted from a foreign body existing in the shadows of our culture, to a central topic across media, households, and individuals. There has never been a time where cannabis was a more frequent topic of conversation than it is now, and I suspect this shift is largely the result of the drastic swings in public perception. People fear what they don't understand, and the truth is that for many years there was much we didn't understand about cannabis. Existing largely as a tool of the black market and the criminal enterprises who profited from it, cannabis arrived in Ziploc bags at high costs and without safety testing. Pesticides ran rampant, human capital was involved in its sale, and the nuances of purity and potency weren't as frequent a topic of discussion due to a lack of access to reliable data. Now, thanks to a large uptick in dialogue resulting from an increasingly regulated *and* legal industry, the black market has begun to fade, products are safe and accessible for those old enough to consume them, and the resulting tax revenue benefits even those who don't. In what feels like the blink of an eye, there is suddenly less to fear.

I tried to look up synonyms for disruption, as I'm sure many are tired of hearing that word tossed around so frequently. There's just no other way to describe what's happening in homes and storefronts all across the country. This new frontier of American business has placed an incredible amount of attention on regulated cannabis markets, and the country is hyper-focused on the impacts of what legalization might bring. Each state that passes meaningful cannabis reform acts as another canary in the coal mine of this great social and economic experiment, all laying the groundwork for the day we think is growing nearer: full federal legalization. When that day does arrive, the hope is that cannabis can join the ranks of all other consumer packaged goods. Our industry's goal is perhaps antithetical to the standard rules of business: *we hope to one day sell a product just like any other.*

INTERVIEW WITH BARRY DILLER

Barry Diller is chairman and senior executive of IAC/InterActivCorp, parent company to household names like Match.com, Tinder, HomeAdvisor, and the Daily Beast, among others. He created the Fox Broadcasting Corporation and USA Broadcasting, and was inducted into the Television Hall of Fame in 1994. Barry is a titan of business and has always found himself ahead of trends. I was fascinated to hear his perspective on an emerging industry and how it compares to the early days of other erstwhile cottage businesses.

You've long been ahead of the curve in emerging markets. Given your track record with spotting trends, where do you see the cannabis industry going in the next twenty years? Some liken it to the dot com boom, and as someone who was on the forefront of that, I'm curious to hear your thoughts on this new and developing market.

There is a lot of potential and a lot of curiosity with the cannabis industry; there have been a lot of legislative advances in the past several years in its favor recently, where the tide has turned. I would liken its progress more to that of the route of marriage equality—a social acceptance issue, as opposed to the dot com bubble, since cannabis is in no way a new phenomenon. Its culture has been around for a very long time. With marriage equality it took some time, state-by-state, for it to become generally accepted (until, of course, the courts set it nationwide), and I think cannabis will closely follow the same path, gradual acceptance–wise—not necessarily with a Supreme Court decision.

The former attorney general for the Trump administration, Jeff Sessions, has made it clear that he is not interested in supporting a regulated cannabis market. What do you think is going to happen on the cannabis issue at the federal level? If not during this administration, then during the next?

I don't think anything will happen at the federal level under this administration; but it's obvious when you now have prominent figures on both sides of the aisle (including the former Speaker of the House and current Senate Majority Leader) investing in the industry and openly supporting and accepting further legalization in some capacity—whether recreationally or medically—that once there is a change in the current leadership, it won't take too much for things to really start moving.

In your view, what responsibility does the media have to its viewers? What I mean is, entertainment value aside, do things like television and film serve some higher purpose beyond sheer entertainment?

To a degree, yes. All media are given an elevated platform, and with that comes an inherent responsibility to hopefully create content for good—whether it be simply for escapism with a mindless TV series, or with more niche documentaries that highlight certain areas of society that needed a megaphone. Especially now, the onus on the industry for encouraging basic civility with its content is important.

How do you see the media being used as a tool for social movements? We've seen it play out with things like #MeToo and in battling for more stringent firearm regulations. What's different about the environment now, that it can create such massive movements seemingly overnight? And is it more difficult now to hear the signal through the noise?

It is more social media than just traditional media. It is very helpful in cases like #MeToo, where this type of bad behavior was happening well before any social media was even around. It was able to be covered up and easily swept under the rug, but now, with such interconnectivity and instant access of information with the platforms, there is very much the mentality of trial by social media, which definitely gives voices and power to movements that never would have been able to speak up before, but likewise can also have damaging consequences if directed with ill intentions. Having all of our current social media platforms, and with such easy access to them, can obviously create these "movements" overnight. More people are engaged and connected, even if passively engaged, than ever before.

When will we see the first cannabis advertisement during the Super Bowl, and what will it take to get there?

I do not think it will be long before that happens. As hard as it is to imagine now, things move quickly and people adapt and accept more easily than we assume.

You're native to LA, a city which, alongside San Francisco, was responsible for creating the first legalized market back in the '90s. What kind of impact do you think regulated cannabis markets have on local economies?

It's very easy to look at Colorado, and now California and other states, and see the impact it has had on communities, the tax earnings alone, which go back into school districts, and local infrastructure, the police and fire departments. It's definitely a rare, new industry that isn't putting the mom-and-pop shops on Main Street out of business. It is important to make sure whatever changes in the industry are done ethically and respectfully, as it's well known the "war on drugs" has disproportionately affected low-income communities and minorities—and to make sure it is not mainstreamed where these corporations come in and profit off of these people whom society has let down and left behind—it should be done with decency at its forefront. The future changes in the cannabis industry could create a real change for the better in our society if done, and regulated, correctly.

CHAPTER 14

O Cann...abis

As the summer of 2018 drew to a close, Canada rolled out full, federal legalization of cannabis, with the vocal support of all-around presidential dreamboat Justin Trudeau. As a red-blooded American, I have a duty to point out that Canada hasn't won a war since 1812, but it can't be denied that they are winning the War on Drugs. And by ushering in a new era of cannabis commoditization, they are setting course to outperform the United States by almost every measure relating to the business of cannabis.

For all the many benefits individual American states have seen as a result of legalizing marijuana in some form, they will be quickly surpassed by Canadian cannabis sales and the resulting tax revenue. Cannabis companies are traded publicly on Canadian stock exchanges, and the government has allowed for cannabis products to be exported to other countries with federally legalized marijuana. Canadians spent $43 million on cannabis in the first two weeks of legalization alone. There is an enormous opportunity that lies ahead for the American people: end the war on cannabis and become a bright, shining example of the power of a regulated market. Federal legalization is about more than tax revenue: It's about access to federal research grants to study the effects of cannabis. It's about creating systems for safe and consistent access, a framework for purchasing cannabis in the light of day. It's about halting the cycle of criminal convictions for a plant that has been deeply embedded in, and increasingly destigmatized by, our culture over the last sixty years. We have to face the facts—we don't have much time, and if we don't act soon, we may be playing catch-up with Canada for years or even decades to come—if we can catch them at all.

All Canadians eighteen and older can rejoice: it's now legal to possess up to thirty grams of dried cannabis flower. Beyond the societal effects of legalization, the Canadian economic model has proven hugely successful for cannabis companies seeking access to public capital. A handful of US cannabis organizations (mine included) have set out to list on Canadian stock exchanges and the results have been astonishing. Aside from the expected volatility of a new commodities trading vertical, these canna-securities have proven to be a hot stock for investors around the world, with companies like Canopy Growth Corporation achieving a $14 billion market cap in short order. Their enormous value is also due in large part to a hefty investment, almost $4 billion, from alcohol giant Constellation Brands, which bolstered their value as a publicly traded Canadian company. It wasn't just a major coup for Canopy Growth, but for the industry as a whole, as it demonstrated real investor appetite in cannabis stocks, and has helped to lay the groundwork for several other companies. Over the past year, we've seen a marked increase in the number of Canadian exchange–listed cannabis brands, each of which offers investors a small taste of what will soon develop into a veritable buffet of publicly traded cannabis businesses.

It's important to take stock of exactly why federal legalization is such a big deal in Canada, in particular when discussing functions of business as they compare to those in the United States. As we know, selling cannabis across state lines (even between two "legal" states) is illegal thanks to the federal status of the plant. The resultant patchwork of laws requires multi-state businesses to set up shop state by state, draining resources and spreading thin many of the smaller companies. Acquiring the resources to replicate and launch distribution and production facilities over and over again across the country is no small feat, and few are able to do it. Meanwhile, in Canada, cannabis moves freely from province to province. What does this look like in practice? Say, for example, that a Canadian cannabis company—let's call them Mountie Marijuana LLC—is cooking up a batch of infused maple bars in their Ontario facility, when their production manager realizes they don't have enough cannabis oil to finish the batch. He (or she—It's 2019, people!) can call up the lab manager at one of their other facilities in another province and simply have the goods couriered over. Easy peasy, right? Now, their American counterpart—let's call them Trumped Up Treats—found themselves cooking up some cannabis-infused, orange (flavored) cookies in a Los Angeles facility. The production manager at Trumped Up Treats realizes that the strain of cannabis they need, Orange Kush, is only available some 1,000 miles away in Denver. If the production manager just made a call to a Colorado grower and had the cannabis shipped out to California, he would be committing a federal crime. So instead, he'd need to find a licensed grow facility in California, contract them to hunt down this specific strain, pay them to grow it, wait six to nine months for the plants to mature, dry, and be processed, and *then* Trumped Up Treats would finally have access to the cannabis required to produce their cookies within the confines of state and federal law. Sounds complicated, right? That's because it is. It hinders a business's ability to be competitive because many products are only allowed to be sold in one state. Our company operates independent labs and extraction facilities (eleven at last count) across the country, serving only the consumers that reside in each respective state. The name of the game is federal compliance, and anyone who wants to survive in the cannabis industry must abide by those rules. We've seen this result in cannabis shortages in some markets and skyrocketing prices in others. Not only is the system needlessly complex, it's inefficient, expensive, and a poor use of a company's resources when the alternative is simple: centralized production facilities that create cannabis products that can be sold all across the country. It works for Amazon, it works for Starbucks, and it would work for the cannabis industry, just as soon as federal law enters the twenty-first century.

Late last year, global business consulting firm Deloitte issued a white paper on the future of cannabis in Canada, a signal of changing tides in itself. They posit that at least two thirds of Canadian marijuana sales will come from legal sources, thanks to an increased consumer demand for tightly regulated products rooted in safety and science. One of their most fascinating observations occurred with regard to the changing demographics of the cannabis consumer of tomorrow. While they found "Risk Takers" aged eighteen to thirty-four make up the bulk of current cannabis purchasers in Canada, Deloitte expects to see a significant shift across the board. "The likely cannabis user," as they describe it, would largely fall under an umbrella known as "The Conservative Experimenter," who is thirty-five to fifty-four years old and uses cannabis less than once a month. Their position is an interesting one because I suspect it illustrates something that's already brewing under the surface in the United States: a shifting demographic that will alter the future of the cannabis space. While products for younger generations tend to focus on getting supremely high, full stop, products aimed at an older generation focus largely on the benefits of consumption—with marketing efforts promoting better sleep and improved mood, for instance.

Even the average observer can begin to see the massive shifts occurring across global cannabis markets: Canada, the first G7 nation to legalize cannabis, and the United States, having failed to enact federal cannabis reform, now exist on a spectrum. Only time will tell how things will shake out for our neighbor to the north but, unlike *The Real Housewives of Toronto*, I suspect they will see massive success.

Meanwhile, in the United States, a new political regime took power in tandem with Canada's legalization efforts, and the result sent a shiver down the spines of cannabis consumers and entrepreneurs alike. In early 2017, with the inauguration of President Trump, the future of cannabis was an unavoidable topic of discussion. His appointment of Jefferson Beauregard Sessions III as attorney general seemed like the death knell for the American cannabis industry. Just say his name out loud and you can tell what his opinion on cannabis would be. When pressed on cannabis consumption, Sessions stated, "Good people don't smoke marijuana."

Within months of his appointment, Sessions had called for the repeal of the Rohrabacher-Farr amendment, a vital piece of legislation to the cannabis industry. In a nutshell, the Rohrabacher-Farr amendment, part of the December 2014 "Cromnibus" Bill signed into law by then-President Barack Obama, was the first real signal from the federal government that cannabis businesses would become off-limits from federal prosecution. The language in the bill barred Justice Department officials from using federal funds to prosecute cannabis businesses operating legally in their respective states. It was first introduced on the floor of the House of Representatives in 2001, but failed to pass six times prior to its success in 2014. When it was finally signed into law, it came with bipartisan support, a rarity for a bill of this kind, and garnered ayes from forty-nine Republicans.

In January 2018, Sessions penned a letter to Congress asking for repeal of the amendment, a move criticized by John Hudak of the Brookings Institution as nothing more than "a scare tactic." During this period, and prior to the approval of the 2019 appropriations budget, many in the cannabis industry felt that this new era of political power could very well be the demise of the cannabis industry as we knew it. Many now regard Sessions' effort as little more than saber rattling against an industry that, as it turns out, is not easily dissuaded by the dated political rhetoric of officeholders. That same month, Sessions, who thought the KKK was "okay until [he] found out they smoked pot," had rescinded the Cole Memorandum, another important layer of protection for the cannabis industry, which advised federal prosecutors not to bring charges against marijuana operations existing in compliance with state and local laws. Once again, the fate of the industry hung in the balance, as the fact that cannabis had largely existed in only a quasi-legal arena for the past decade became glaringly apparent.

It's easy, of course, to lose track of the fact that what we do is still a federal crime. I'm certainly guilty of it, and it's due in large part to the circumstances of my surroundings. Having spent the bulk of my adult life in either Los Angeles or Denver, I tend to forget how high the stakes are in the rest of the country. My paychecks are issued by ADP. I use an American Express corporate card when taking clients out to lunch or buying office supplies. We work out of a beautiful office in downtown Denver, have a huge team across the country, and operate in much the same way as any other business. You can understand, then, how we could forget. It wasn't until Jeff Sessions took office that this realization leaped from the shadows and beat the hell out of me. Anxious uncertainty plagued the industry for several months. For the most part, however, business went on as usual—assuming we don't count my increased levels of palm sweat. There was no point in changing anything unless the feds were actually going to take action against our community. By late November 2018, like so many of the President's Best People™, Sessions *stepped down* from his position, and the industry unclenched its collective buttocks. Cannabis stocks shot up as much as 30 percent on news of the resignation. The industry would live to see another day.

Behind the scenes, there is growing support in the US political system for regulated cannabis. The Congressional Cannabis Caucus, founded in 2017 by Republicans Dana Rohrabacher and Don Young, along with Democrats Earl Blumenauer and Jared Polis, Colorado's current governor, quickly attracted bipartisan support. Now entering its second term, the group demonstrates the seriousness with which many politicians are approaching the industry. At the time of writing, Polis and Rohrabacher are no longer in office and have been replaced by Democrat Barbara Lee and Republican David Joyce. Beyond that, a 2017 Gallup poll found that 51 percent of Republican voters now support legalization, up a full *nine percentage points* from 2016. While we may differ a great deal in terms of progress when compared with our neighbor to the north, the changing tides in American opinion have never been more apparent.

I was recently in Florida—a state notorious in the industry for its arcane regulations—working with a group of prospective partners. At the end of a long day, we found ourselves sitting in a stereotypical country club at the end of a tree-lined road. We spent the evening discussing the potential impact of legalization, when a man from a neighboring table decided to chime in. Here we were, sitting deep in the Florida suburbs, at a large table inside the physical embodiment of "can't teach an old dog new tricks," when a man who was comfortably ninety years old wanted to chat about the merits of cannabis. He was a fan.

With the twenty-four-hour news cycle, it's easy to get caught up in the "green rush" narrative and persuade ourselves that the people of the world have already changed their minds. The truth is, it's in these small, human moments that the changing tides are most evident. It's the grandfather in the South Florida country club that marks the beginning of great social change, not the *Forbes* headline or the political endorsements. The latter two still carry a great deal of weight, but ultimately the success of those with political power is based largely on the opinions of their constituents. Given that, it stands to reason that as individual voters are exposed to more and more information about cannabis, they begin to ask the right questions of their representatives, and the winds of political opinion begin to change. It's a slow process to be sure, but I'm hard pressed to think of one happening in shorter order than the movement we have before us now. This social movement boils down to a simple question. At the end of the day, how many other industries broadly excite the masses, inspire investors, and offer social clout to politicians?

For all the pomp and circumstance surrounding federal cannabis laws, the simple reality is that none of it should really matter to the Senators and Congressmen most staunchly opposed to it. From where I'm standing, it boils down to a state's rights issue, and unless the long arm of justice pushes the death penalty for those involved in cannabis, the industry will live on. In 1995, Justice Anthony Kennedy wrote that:

> *Federalism was our Nation's own discovery. The Framers split the atom of sovereignty. It was the genius of their idea that our citizens would have two political capacities, one state and one federal, each protected from incursion by the other. The resulting Constitution created a legal system unprecedented in form and design, establishing two orders of government, each with its own direct relationship, its own privity, its own set of mutual rights and obligations to the people who sustain it and are governed by it.*

Perhaps the greatest irony of the still-lingering conservative distaste for cannabis is that the most-asserted value held by American flag pin–wearing Republicans *is* states' rights. The split atom, as Kennedy argued, is a tenant held as one of the most vital pieces of modern politics.

When it comes to cannabis, however, this ideology has been largely ignored. While cannabis has been allowed at various state levels for the better part of thirty years, it has been in near-constant conflict with federal regulators. From Jeff Sessions to Paul Ryan, Republicans at the highest levels have largely ignored state's rights when it comes to the treatment of cannabis. Even at a state level, according to a recent NORML scorecard of newly elected governors, only five of twenty-four Republicans received above a "C" grade when it came to their policy on cannabis reform. Perhaps the most perplexing aspect of this discord lies in the double-standard of criminal prosecution. With the rescinding of the Cole Memorandum, it's been made clear that when it comes to cannabis, states' rights come second, despite public support in favor of cannabis. There are a few different factors at play here, and they are ones largely shared by any successful industry. For one, people love it. If nationwide sales of cannabis (both legal and illegal) tell us anything, it's that this booming industry fills a void in the hearts and minds of consumers across the country. For those fortunate enough to live in regulated markets, the money is just too good to walk away from. New Frontier Data, a leading analytics firm, predicts that federal tax revenue from cannabis could reach $132 billion dollars, and the industry will create over a million jobs by 2022, assuming federal legalization takes place in the near future. Cannabis *is* the next great American industry. Unlike former blue chip companies such as Kodak or General Motors, who saw dramatic downturns as a result of changing technology, cannabis is *enabled* to thrive as a result of technological changes. And just for icing on the cake (or weed in the joint), there's always a built-in market for substances that alter our collective state of mind. If we've learned anything from alcohol and tobacco companies, it's that these two industries are the only ones to see an uptick in sales during periods of economic depression. It's common sense—people like to get fucked up.

For all the political rhetoric around job creation in this country, it seems that cannabis has largely been ignored as the solution to this problem. Take coal, for example. What was once one of the largest industries in the country now offers just under 50,000 full-time jobs. Then there are one-time giants like Eastman Kodak Company, which employed some 120,000 people in 1973 but now has just 5,000 after a tumultuous bankruptcy. Industry health is reflective of demand, and as a result of changes in technology or consumer trends, many companies that were once thought to be untouchable have collapsed.

One of the biggest misconceptions of the cannabis industry is that the only people who benefit from it are the ones who directly touch the plant. The truth is, indirect job creation is one of the key byproducts of the industry, lauded by proponents of legalization. Breaking it down into two groups, direct and indirect, some 200,000 people are gainfully employed in cannabis-adjacent jobs across the country. This figure, according to New Frontier Data, is set to triple by 2025. By 2021, cannabis legalization will create one job for every 1,000 Americans, according to that same study. Though it's hard to find exact figures, it's useful to run through the list of jobs that are either created or bolstered as a result of cannabis legalization. Starting at a high level, any functioning business will need to employ some combination of accountants, attorneys, compliance consultants, corporate recruiters, human resources firms, and outside advertising agencies and partners. Moving down the scale, there are the companies that produce grow lights, hoses, light bulbs, hardware for extraction technology; manufacturers; fertilizer and nutrient companies; soil producers; and even city public works employees, who set up and monitor new commercial utilities. There are packaging manufacturers, outside public relations firms who help share messaging on behalf of these companies, and vendors who fill offices with soft drinks, snacks, and catering. Airline travel for many cannabis companies rivals that of even some *Fortune* 500s, as the global nature of our business warrants a great deal of movement. There are office supplies, batch labels, telecommunications companies, commercial software licenses, technology purchases, and Point of Sale systems. Real estate markets are bolstered as dispensaries and cannabis brands alike move into vacant retail and office spaces, lovingly decorated by interior designers contracted for the job. Armored cars carry funds from store to bank, and testing facilities are bustling with cannabis products waiting to pass muster with state regulators.

Cannabis is about more than just growing weed—it's about putting Americans back to work, with projects they can believe in. We're living in a new era—let's call it the Great Disruption—and it's cannabis that is leading the pack.

The ideology ultimately boils down to a few simple questions: Do you support ending the illegal black market? Do you want to see Americans working in high-paying jobs, even without a college degree? Are you in support of ending the war on cannabis and the mass incarcerations of people of color? If the answer to any of the above is a resounding *yes*, then you support the federal legalization of cannabis. There's no gray area here—legalized cannabis is coming, and if we've learned anything from Canada, the Earth won't fall to pieces around us when it happens. So, the question stands, when the War on Drugs ends, will you be standing on the right side of history? The time for reform is now, and without direct and meaningful action, we run the risk of regressing to a time when cannabis-use was akin to siding with the devil. American industries are suffering: auto manufacturers are taking record hits on the stock market, coal jobs are being replaced by clean energy, and technological innovations have made many once-stable careers now obsolete. The answer is here and the answer is clear: choose cannabis.

INTERVIEW WITH JEREMY HEIDL

Jeremy Heidl is the cofounder and executive vice president of product at Organa Brands. Along with his wife and two other partners, Jeremy launched its predecessor, O.penVAPE in 2012, creating what would soon become the largest distributer of cannabis products in America. He is an ardent supporter of creativity in the workplace, encouraging members of his team to follow his lead and think outside of the box at all times. I spoke with Jeremy to learn more about his commitment to company culture and what role disruption plays in creating it.

When did you first know you'd come across something different?

The first couple of times I heard a patient say something like "I'm not having seizures anymore," or "I'm off the painkillers," I realized that we were, without a doubt, on the right side of a cultural change. I'm not a doctor and I haven't had a debilitating condition, but I can't argue with the hundred of consumers I've met over the last decade that have explained the difference cannabis has made in their lives.

What industry is the most similar to cannabis, and in what way?

The most frequent comparisons I see are to liquor or pharma or even tobacco, but what I've experienced is more *authentic* than any of those spaces. In a lot of ways, all industries are somewhat similar...this widget and that widget. Perhaps the most unique aspect of the cannabis business is the people that are drawn to working in it. They are renegades and rule breakers, they tend to be of above-average intelligence (if I do say so myself), and they're just generally chaotic-but-resilient get-shit-done-rs!

How do you balance the risk vs. reward of being in such a novel industry?

There's a huge disparity between the *perceived* risk in the cannabis industry and the *actual* risk. Therein lies the opportunity. Perhaps most surprising is that I've never lost sleep over the possibility of federal drug enforcement. I'm more concerned about inconsistent regulations (280e being a great example) and their side effects.

What does disruption mean in the context of your job?

Perpetual evolution. Good is never good enough.

Does that disruption carry over into a company's culture? And what, in your eyes, is the importance of that company culture?

Absolutely it carries over. One of our core values is "we support good mistakes," so our team is able to try various approaches and take certain calculated risks that you might not expect from relatively young professionals. As long as there is a best effort put forward, even if there is a negative end-result, we learn from it and move on. When you have a culture that supports disruption and perpetual evolution over the "analysis paralysis" of budget drills, you can make a mistake and get it right more quickly, often before your competition gives it their first shot. *Just make a decision.*

You mentioned chaos earlier—what place does measured chaos have in a workplace? And how does it contribute to more creative thought and innovation?

Chaos is motion—not always in the right direction, to be sure—but exploring boundaries through controlled chaos promotes the disruption and perpetual evolution we discussed. Chaos is also addictive, which works for the right team, especially creative types.

What's the most important lesson you've learned over the years about the value of culture and its role in creating a sustainable, long-term brand?

The most important lesson has been how significant the relationship is between our company's culture and the perception of our brands. What and who we are as an organization is reflected in our brands and it really couldn't be any other way. Our brands are as authentic as each of the individuals in our company, and I'm certain, especially in the cannabis industry, that a shift in our underlying culture would inevitably shift the perception of our company that's held by our retail partners and consumers.

CHAPTER 15

The Myth of Two Roads

Cannabis has never been scarcer. The black market is thriving. Those in need of alternatives for pain relief are left without non-pharmaceutical options. On the street, a gram of weed sells for thirty-five dollars—if you're lucky enough to find some grown locally, it may cost double that. Crime rates across the country have increased, due in large part to the recession that hit the country some years earlier. American unemployment rates are at a forty-year high, and nearly all of our goods are imported, especially drugs. The human capital associated with the purchase of marijuana has also increased markedly, as violence in the Southwest grows to unprecedented levels, thanks in large part to the trafficking of marijuana over, under, and across the border. The DEA has been tasked with protecting our citizens from themselves, and what few mom-and-pop cannabis growing operations remain get raided before their seeds hit the soil. Schools and highways are in disrepair, an infrastructure bill never getting the votes for passage. Inside prison walls, record numbers of inmates serve life sentences for nonviolent cannabis charges. Families are ripped apart, and the private prison economy thrives off of their suffering. The year is 2022.

To the north, Canada is the biggest exporter of cannabis, which is largely responsible for their top economic position in the G7. Hundreds of thousands of Canadians are gainfully employed within the cannabis industry, and the country has seen a marked drop in crime and underage use. Thanks to government research grants, Canada leads the charge in the development of CBD and THC-based pharmaceutical applications. To the south, Mexico, having legalized recreational marijuana, is putting a dent in the years-long cartel war that has left countless dead. Their economy is booming, with tourists from around the world coming to enjoy a tropical vacation with a joint in hand.

This could be our future if we don't move quickly on a new cannabis policy in this country.

According to a 2018 piece in *Newsweek*:

Almost half of corporate CFOs, 49 percent, say the US economy's decade-long growth streak is set to collide with worsening debt woes, with the country facing a recession by the end of next year. Corporate finance leaders are preparing for the recession to hit within 18 months, and 82 percent of CFOs interviewed in the latest quarterly Duke University/CFO Global Business Outlook survey expect the US to slide into a recession by 2020.

There are many reasons that this economic downturn may be looming, but the jury is still out on when we might expect to see the shift. The volatility of the stock market in late 2018 has been discussed as perhaps the first warning sign of what's to come. Perhaps one area most to blame for the imbalance of power on the global scale is our seeming inability to stay ahead of the curve in various industrial verticals. Take car manufacturing as an example. What was once the cornerstone of American industry, US auto manufacturing has been largely outperformed by foreign companies. Japan's Toyota Camry is the bestselling car of 2018 in the United States. When it comes to the development of new technology, Silicon

Valley is lauded as the world hub for innovation. That said, most of the technology created in California is produced overseas and imported into the United States. According to a new study from the Institute for Health Metrics and Evaluation, the United States ranks number twenty-seven in terms of both healthcare and education. Pew Research found that the US ranks number thirty-eight out of seventy-one in mathematical proficiency.

A recent study in the *Economic Journal* found that border states with legalized cannabis, like California and New Mexico, have seen a drop of almost 13 percent in violent crimes, yet another testament to the benefits of legalization. This decrease is largely a result of lessening drug traffic into the aforementioned states, where cannabis that's grown in Mexico for seventy-five dollars per pound will sell for over $6,000 once it make its way into the US, the *Guardian* found. Meanwhile, the opioid epidemic plaguing our country takes the lives of 130 Americans each day. According to NIDA, some 30 percent of those prescribed opioids will abuse them. In the late 1990s, drug companies made assurances that these products were not addictive, and the resulting over-prescription of opioid painkillers has led to one of the worst public health emergencies in modern history. Another NIDA study found that in 2015, two million Americans suffered from opioid addiction, and of those, 33,000 died from overdoses. At least 6 percent of those using opioids will transition to heroin use in their lifetime. This is thanks, in large part, to the lower cost and easy access to heroin, which often serves as a bridge between a lack of prescription opioids and the high that they deliver. Meanwhile, cannabis has proven to be an effective method of harm-reduction for those who may otherwise have no alternative to prescription painkillers. In a 2012 study in the *Harm Reduction Journal*, Mark Collen cited research that the total costs of prescription opioid abuse totaled $8.1 billion, including police resources and subsidized medical costs, while the cost to police cannabis use was $7.7 billion per year. Between 1999 and 2009, the same study found that hospital admissions for opioid overdose increased 516 percent. The study concludes with the author's opinion that cannabis, when administered effectively, can be beneficial to patients as a first-line defense for chronic pain prior to starting opioid therapy. Around the world, between twenty-six and thirty-six million people suffer from opioid addiction, according to a 2018 study from Beth Wiese and Adrianne R. Wilson-Poe of Washington University. Perhaps not shockingly, their research found that of those currently prescribed opioids, 40–60 percent of patients will reduce their opioid use when given cannabis as an alternative. Further, they found that the use of cannabis can reduce opioid withdrawal symptoms, a possible solution to the staggering rates of opioid relapse—estimated at 80 percent for opioid addicts trying to quit.

There is an alternative to the possible future I detailed above. Just within reach is a future that brings our drug policies into the twenty-first century and passes legislation at a federal level in order to fix the cannabis problem in our country. If you were to present this to a freshman English major, they would tell you that there are two roads diverging in the green wood before us. Popular opinion has largely swung in favor of cannabis in the last five years, marking a shift in the minds of voters across the country. There will be a turning point, sometime soon, when so few Americans oppose cannabis legalization, that the federal government is left with no option but to legalize it. That future, where cannabis is the greatest new industry in modern history, is the one on which I dwell.

New Frontier Data posits that if federal legalization were to occur, the government would see a $138 billion uptick in aggregate tax revenue by 2025. This increase could fundamentally alter the landscape of our country. The question is, how would we spend it? We could offer free college education at state institutions for anyone who wanted it—that would eat up about half of the cannabis taxes brought in, roughly $70 billion. In a 2012 piece from the *New York Times* citing a Department of Housing and Urban Development study, a $20 billion per year appropriation would effectively end homelessness across the country. Or, assuming these projections for this potential tax revenue aren't far off the mark, we could easily cover the estimated $26 billion it would cost to offer universal pre-K. I know that there are many out there who are still put off by the notion of legalizing cannabis from sea to shining sea and the impact it could have on society as a whole. Here, I tug at the heartstrings of federal budget hawks—if you can't support cannabis, you can at least support increased balances in the federal coffers. How the potential revenue is ultimately allocated, I can't say, but I'm hard pressed to think of an instance where an influx of some $130 billion couldn't be put to good use.

We've seen the ripple effect that cannabis job creation sparks, leading to more and better jobs for those involved on even the fringes of this new world. From lighting manufacturers to fertilizer companies, cannabis creates jobs and puts Americans to work. Gone are the days of the American auto-industry boom, and along with them many of the skilled labor jobs that once fueled our economy. What's left, right here, right now, is an opportunity to rewrite the future, and create a prosperous sector of the American job market that's rooted in, well, roots. This plant has proven to not only be an effective social lubricant, but a substance of huge import to the medical community, as well as a stimulus to the economy. The choice, for me at least, is clear. Cannabis may not solve all of our problems, but it's the the most lucrative option we have at the moment.

It's now early 2019, and I've been living in Denver for the last six months, marking a return to where it all began. The world is a different place than it was when I first walked in the doors to my job in the cannabis industry, but in many ways it's much the same. The amount of work still left to do is often daunting, but it's never boring or unrewarding. As the director of public relations for one of the largest cannabis companies in the country, I've been lucky to get to make up a lot of the rules as I go along, forging a path for those who will come after me, those who will improve upon my work and hopefully learn from my mistakes (don't wear skinny jeans to a political fundraiser, for example). The current political climate may well throw our livelihood into question, but so far quite the opposite has taken place, and most of us have never been more certain of the future that's to come.

To the north, the sky hasn't fallen, and a federally legal cannabis program will likely prove to be one of the most daring social experiments of our lifetime, serving as a catalyst for the western world to finally put a stop to a century of failed drug policy. Here in America, cannabis has never been more *in*. From restaurants to hotels, to conversations with grandparents and distant cousins, cannabis has had a dramatic shift in its standing within the confines of society. Gone are the days of hushed dealings in darkly lit rooms. Cannabis now lives in the light. Not only does it live, but just like the plant itself, *it thrives* in the light. The shift in popular opinion has pushed cannabis into the zeitgeist, making it a staple of what it means to be modern. Where cracking a beer at the end of the day once served as the ultimate American pastime, it is slowly being edged out by its botanical cousin. Science is starting to catch up with anecdotal claims, and we see dramatic shifts in the perception of the role of cannabis in medicine. In my own life, I forgot what it was like to live in a place where cannabis is king. Denver is a bustling metropolitan city, a far departure from the podunk western outpost that existed here decades prior. Streets are clean, schools are being built, and every corner is dotted with the mystical green cross, a distinctly American symbol of good times ahead.

The walk from my apartment to work is a short one, and on the way, a piece of paper gets stuck to my shoe. I bend down to pick it up. It's a flyer for a cannabis convention happening the following week. The organizers boast of access to institutional investors looking to hear pitches from cannabis up-and-comers. The doors to the modern system of business—which used to be slammed in our face—have swung open, greeting cannabis entrepreneurs with a warm embrace that can only be explained by the vast potential this industry has proven to possess. I peel the flyer from my shoe and toss it into the trash. Inside the bin, there's a wrapper for one of our products—just another reminder that what we do for a living has far-reaching effects outside the four walls of our office. None of us got into cannabis because we had any degree of confidence that we'd one day change the world—but it's happened. I try to remind myself every day just how small I am in the time line of humanity and the sheer vastness of our universe, but in some ways, I revel in the idea that I've played some small role in the changing of the guard—the shift in perception that's begun to pave the way for an America, for a world, where cannabis isn't a bad word, but rather a tool for a new generation of disruptors. The ones who see what needs fixing and who work tirelessly to change it—from drug policy reform, to ensuring safe access, to paying social and fiscal reparations to the victims of the War on Drugs. The cannabis industry isn't going anywhere—our collective heels have been dug in, and the only thing that will change is society.

Like any great social movement, ours has been fraught with discord and confusion, uncertainty and excitement. The new era of cannabis serves as a reminder of what is possible when a group of outsiders bands together. Our demands, on their own, are few: legalize cannabis and allow a new industry to flourish. I don't think it's asking too much. We owe social dues to this new industry—to create something powerful and to ensure its development is both responsible and sustainable. In a time filled with divisiveness, I can think of few better causes to unite us than this one. I don't work for a marijuana company because I like to get high or because I identify with the culture. The real connection here is the humanistic one, the idea that we can help people, change the world, and reshape many facets of our country for years to come. Cannabis is here to stay.

I never explained what happened in the weeks before going to rehab, and I don't think I ever will. Addiction makes people do tragic, demoralizing things. I still find some comfort in my old ways of living. When things are difficult at work, or when I'm tossing in bed at night worried about the day to come, I snuggle up to my old ways of thinking like a familiar blanket from childhood. It only takes a moment before reality sets back in, however, and I'm reminded of just how lonely that time in my life was. Surrounded by friends and family, a job that I loved, and stacked social calendar, I'd never been more alone. That's the brutal fact of living a double life: no one really knows you. Sure, the relationships are real and so is the love, but when I came out the other side, things needed to be rebuilt from scratch. A lot of people still don't understand what led me down the path of addition. I don't fully understand it either. What I do know is that I learned to lie from a very young age. In the small town where I grew up in the '90s, a confused gay kid had no choice but to lie. "I'm fine" should have been my yearbook quote. It's an eerie feeling to return to my hometown with a man who I love proudly and out in the open. It's the antithesis of my old life—a life where I hid every piece of my innermost self, leaving only shreds of the truth clawing at the inside of my throat in search of a way out. This emotional masquerade, enabled me to become an expert at a secret addiction. I could teach a masterclass on how to hide the truth and simply act as if there was nothing amiss, but what would be the point in teaching anyone those skills? It's lonely there. It offers nothing but a knot in the stomach, a pain that can only be relieved by unsavory solutions and characters. In the search for some semblance of peace, we often incite chaos—at least that was the case with me. A half a decade of therapy later, I don't recognize the person in the photos prior to sobriety. It doesn't look like me. It doesn't feel like me. I didn't expect to end up with the job I have or the life I've built, but if all this time working with weed has taught me anything, it's that things only grow in the light.

I sit on the couch in the apartment where I live with my husband and our dog. Just outside the window, half a block away, is the beaux-arts apartment complex in which I used to live. I'd swear it was yesterday and a lifetime ago. I can see the roof I nearly leapt from four years ago. Things are different now. I laugh to myself when I think about my byline—"sober weed dealer."

All due respect to Robert Frost, the idea of "two roads" is bull-shit. There are never *just* two roads. Take it from me—if you find yourself wandering a wood and are forced to choose between two seemingly identical paths, it's time to pull out a machete and forge your own.

Acknowledgments

One morning, on a typically hot and humid day in Puerto Rico, I woke up with an idea for a book. I told Michael about the idea, and in his usual style, he replied with a simple, "You should do it." Of course, neither of us had any idea what I would be getting into, but one of the greatest parts of our relationship is that we both just enjoy the ride. So to Michael: Thank you for supporting me throughout the late nights, the long weekends, and both the metaphorical and literal breakdowns that went along with creating this book. I love you, and I couldn't have done any of this without you.

To the cofounders of SLANG Worldwide: Chris Driessen, Jeremy Heidl, Chris McElvany, John Moynan, Billy Levy, and Peter Miller— thank you for letting me tell the story of not just this groundbreaking company, but the incredible industry we are all so lucky to be able to participate in. Additionally, I owe a debt of gratitude for not only your participation in this book, but for your patience in allowing me to write it. I owe a particularly heavy thanks to Jeremy Heidl, Chris Driessen, and Chris McElvany for taking a chance on a college kid with no idea what he was getting into when I stumbled through our office doors five years ago. And speaking of stumbling—the life I have now, a sober one, is thanks to the kindness, concern, and love that each of you showed to me during a dark period in my life. Your compassion allowed me to get the help I needed, and I'm a better man because of it.

To my beloved friends and colleagues at Creative Artists Agency, namely Nick "From the Hamptons" Thimm, thank you for your friendship, and for introducing me to my unbelievable agent, Cait Hoyt. Cait, without you, this book would be nothing more than an ill-fated idea. You've played therapist, mentor, advisor, and most importantly, friend. Thank you for tolerating the barrage of emails, late-night calls, and fits of tears. I would be lost without you. Of course, thanks are also in order to my friend Alexa "Swim Swim Swim" Cook, for taking a meeting four years ago with a cannabis company that had a wild idea for a stadium name. As you put it, "All the feels." Additional thanks to Jamie Stockton, Norris Brooks, Emily Westcott, and the rest of the team at CAA who helped make this book a reality. Lastly, thank you to Carla Laur, my first friend in Los Angeles. If it weren't for our first meeting, I would have never wound up in the CAA family.

The man behind the book, Jacob Hoye at Post Hill Press. Thank you for guiding me through uncharted territory, and for doing so with kindness and patience—two requirements for a particularly neurotic first-time author. Your words of encouragement and unfaltering dedication to this book have been nothing short of amazing. Thank you to Anthony Ziccardi for taking a chance on me and letting this project come to life. Finally, thank you to Heather King and the rest of the team at Post Hill Press, your hard work and enthusiasm has not gone unnoticed.

To my talented and wonderful friend Ellen Bruss at EBD: Thank you from the bottom of my heart for bringing the pages of this book to life. Your years of friendship have been a blessing. A special thanks as well to Ken Garcia, Jessie James, and the rest of the team at EBD. Your artistic vision and creative minds have created something that jumps off the shelf.

A heartfelt thank you to all those who provided insights and interviews. Without your participation, this book would be little more than hyperbole: Daryn Carp, Peter Davis, "Dr." Dina Browner,

Stephanie Landa, Austin Carlisle, Tracie Morrissey, and Robin Abcarian. Special thanks to Barry Diller, for not only offering unparalleled insights about the landscape of business in America, but for being a great ally and resource over the years for an endless number of wild ideas.

To my colleagues and friends in Puerto Rico: Jamie Meyer, Amanda von Heidl, Akida Johnson, Mike Eckles, Brittany Hallett, and Weston Brown, thank you for tolerating my constant discussion of this book when it was not more than an idea in an email.

To Annie Fay, thank you for your critical eye in the creation of this book, and for being a guiding light in the premise and structure of the complex ideas that I set out to tackle. Beyond that, thank you for your years of friendship, for keeping me sane in the early days, and for being my fellow food-snob, who's never given more than a seven out of ten rating to any restaurant in the greater Los Angeles area. You're a unicorn.

To my lifelong friends, Caroline Connelly, Madison Konner, Perry Bradley, Gabbie Mehan, Danielle Sexton, Delilah Vigil, Hillary Mork, Kerry Holihan, Justin Horstmann, Emily Weiland, Matt Glassett, and Emily Cavanagh: I love each of you more than words can express and can't thank you enough for your support and friendship over the last decade.

It's with love and adoration that I thank Barbie Rosenberg, for inviting me into her home in Los Angeles when I had little more than a month of sobriety, and nurturing me back to health with love and friendship. You saved my life, and I will never be able to thank you enough for it. Great thanks are also in order for the team who got me sober in the first place, namely Bianca Rodriguez, Patricia Meyers, and the world-class team of professionals at Promises Malibu.

Thank you, of course, to my mentors and friends who have carefully guided me in different ways over the years, but most importantly, have never asked for anything in return. To Jill Dupre, for your years of mentoring and friendship, to Siva Vaidhyanathan for first sparking my obsession with media and society and inspiring me to become an author in the first place, and to Joshua Weinstein, who not only guides me in all matters of spirituality and the pursuit of happiness, but who introduced me to the love of my life and changed us for the better. Thank you as well to Julia Lynne, Courtney Luce, and Barbara Opp, who taught me what it means to write. Gaylen McQuown—even though I can't paint to save my life, I know good art when I see it thanks to you. To Sir Michael Fay, for allowing me to feel at home on Great Mercury Island, and for whose wisdom and friendship I am forever grateful. Thank you as well for the great privilege of allowing me the use of your private office to take the call from Cait that this book had been sold. Thank you also to Ann Dickerson, who took a PR novice under her wing, and helped turn me into a professional.

To my family, Mary, Dave, and Cole Tilley, who raised me with nothing less than absolute and unconditional love. I am who I am because of you. Everything I have, I owe to you and your sacrifices. Without our family, I am nothing. To my grandmother, "Meme" Shirley Carney, there are no words to express what it means to have a friendship like ours. It's because of you that I have a love of books, of critical thought, and of anything that airs on MSNBC. You are my first best friend, and this book is for you. To the Maranos, thank you for welcoming me into your family with love and open arms. Michael, Shelia, Bennett, Alex, and Kelsey, it is a privilege to call you family. Thank you as well to Shelby and Taylor Coon, for sharing my love of all things bougie, and for reminding me that I hit the in-law jackpot.

Finally, thank you to Bobby Kennedy, our Cavalier King Charles Spaniel. Without your lazy eyes and obsession with loose string, there would be less joy in the world.